Signed

# TITANIC
# – the Norfolk
# Survivors

To Bernard,
with best wishes,
John Bells,
June, 1999.

To Sylvia, Richard and Alison
… and in grateful memory of
Frank, Ethel, Edward,
Ellen and May

# TITANIC
## – the Norfolk Survivors

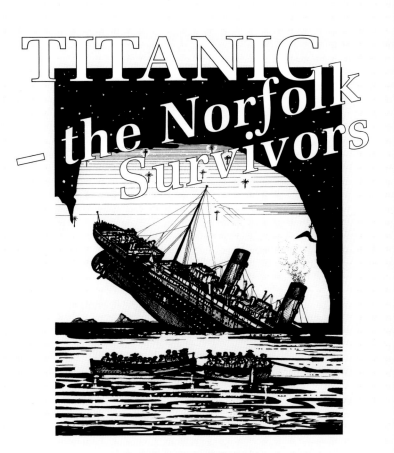

## John Balls

Publications

TOFTWOOD · DEREHAM · NORFOLK

*Published by:*
NOSTALGIA PUBLICATIONS
(Terry Davy)
7 Elm Park, Toftwood,
Dereham, Norfolk
NR19 1NB


*First impression:* March 1999


© John Balls


ISBN 0 947630 25 2

*Design and typesetting:*
NOSTALGIA PUBLICATIONS


*Printed by:*
BARNWELL'S OF AYLSHAM
Penfold Street,
Aylsham, Norfolk,
NR11 6ET

# Contents

# Acknowledgements

I am grateful for the assistance of a number of people in this project.

The members of the Norfolk Titanic Association have encouraged me with their interest, and I have received a great deal of help from the relatives of local survivors, especially Gladys Whitworth, Edward (John) Clarke, Betty Terrell, Sue Roberson and Irene Rhodes. In my search in Old Buckenham for information concerning Ellen Bird I have gained greatly from the support of Thora Lindenmayer. Craig Stringer, an expert on the Titanic lifeboats' passengers, has dealt with a number of queries. Chris Crowther has given me much assistance in investigating the claim that a *Titanic* lifeboat has been found locally. I have worked with Steve Snelling from the *Eastern Daily Press* on a number of articles and have benefited from this co-operation, and from the help of another journalist, Chris Stokes.

Permission to reproduce photographs has been received from Barnardo's, Nick Walmsley, Eastern Counties Newspapers, Irene Rhodes, the John Lewis Partnership, Clifford Temple, Rex Stevens, Patricia Goreham and Richard Berry.

Sylvia Yates' excellent proof-reading has considerably improved the text. My wife, Sylvia, and my son and daughter, Richard and Alison, have supported and encouraged me in this task, as well as accepting my obsession with the *Titanic*!

*John Balls,*
*Norwich, 1999*

# Introduction

The story of the sinking of the *Titanic* in April 1912 is full of interesting and challenging comparisons and juxtapositions. This was a tragedy on a global scale with international repercussions, yet its fascination is very much the product of the involvement of human beings in this event, human beings from many countries and from all classes of society. This means that, alongside the many books which deal with the wider implications of this event, there is a place for a study of the local and limited impact of the sinking on ordinary people.

This book is an attempt to add an extra dimension to such aspects of the story as the rescue of survivors, the reporting of the event in the local press, and the attempts to raise money to support those left destitute by the tragic loss of life. The search for information concerning the sinking is a never-ending one and I hope that one result of the publication of this book will be the discovery of fresh material concerning the people and events dealt with here.

RMS Titanic in Southampton Water, 10 April 1912, by Nick Walmsley

# Chapter One

# The Sinking of the Titanic

**'SOS. We have struck iceberg.**
**Require assistance.**
**Position 41.46N 50.14W. Titanic.'**

In order to understand the significance of the links between the County of Norfolk and the sinking of the *Titanic*, we need to consider some of the basic facts about the ship - the background to its construction, the maiden voyage and the aftermath of the tragedy. However, many of the so-called 'facts' are in dispute, and new theories to account for what happened are produced at frequent intervals. Much of the fascination which grips so many *Titanic* enthusiasts is the result of the unanswered questions which give rise to so much speculation. My own interest began when studying the poems of Thomas Hardy for examination purposes, and finding there *The Convergence of The Twain*, written in May 1912. In this poem we see Hardy's fondness for dealing with irony, as he contrasts the splendour of the great ship with its sad state at the bottom of the ocean.

*'Over the mirrors meant*
*To glass the opulent*
*The sea-worm crawls - grotesque, slimed, dumb,*
*    indifferent.'*

Hardy talks about the 'Spinner of the Years' who brings together the ship and the iceberg, with a 'consummation' which 'jars two hemispheres'. This points to the global significance of this tragedy which still resounds eighty-seven years after the event. It brought to an end an era in which people felt that science and

**FIRST SAILING OF THE LATEST ADDITION TO THE WHITE STAR FLEET**

## The Queen of the Ocean

# TITANIC

LENGTH 882½ FT.        OVER 45,000 TONS        BEAM 92½ FT.
TRIPLE-SCREWS

This, the Latest, Largest and Finest Steamer Afloat, will sail from

**WHITE STAR LINE, PIER 10, SOUTHAMPTON**

# WEDNESDAY, APRIL 10TH,

## AT 12 NOON

calling at Cherbourg & Queenstown, Co. Cork
*en route to NEW YORK*

Reservations of Berths may be made direct with this Office or through any of our accredited Agents

### THIRD CLASS RATES ARE:

From **SOUTHAMPTON, LONDON, LIVERPOOL** } **£7 : 9s : 0d**

From **QUEENSTOWN** } **£6 : 10s : 0d**

DO NOT DELAY: Secure your tickets through the local Agents or direct from

**WHITE STAR LINE**          •          **ISMAY IMRIE & CO.**
1 Cockspur Street, SW.          88 Leadenhall Street, EC London

*Poster advertising the maiden voyage of the Titanic*

technology could do anything, even to the extent of producing an 'unsinkable' ship. Man's arrogance which leads to carelessness was highlighted, and this was just one of many moral lessons which were taken from the sinking. Stories of heroism and cowardice, of government folly and of corporate greed soon became public property as the legend of the *Titanic* gripped the popular imagination. The fact that the ship carried such a wide range of passengers in terms of nationality and class added to the interest, and this part of the story still provides an important focus for a consideration of what happened. The James Cameron block-buster was not the first film to concentrate on the importance of the class division on the ship, with its potential for a love-story which challenged these assumptions. In deciding to focus on the story of two passengers, Cameron shows that in dealing with such an enormous event it is often necessary to reduce the scale to something which we as individuals can comprehend. He decided to use fictitious characters, but as we look at the story we must never lose sight of the fact that they were real people there on the deck of that ship at midnight on 14 April 1912. My own interest in the *Titanic* has been centred on the human beings involved, rather than on the technical aspects of the ship and the sinking. This has led me to my investigation of the stories of the Norfolk survivors.

In the late nineteenth century the commercial possibilities of providing transport across the Atlantic had become obvious in their potential for making money. The advent of steam-driven ships had reduced crossing-times to the extent that holiday and business travel was attractive to Americans; this increased a trade which was already lucrative in providing transport for the many Europeans who saw emigration to the United States as their only real opportunity of escaping from the poverty trap in which they found themselves. Competition was immense, and one of the leading players was the White Star Line. This had been purchased by Thomas Henry Ismay in 1867 and his first task was to set about establishing the Company as a high-class steamship service in the Atlantic passenger trade. His son, J. Bruce Ismay, had taken over after his father's death in 1899. Three years later the White Star Line was purchased by the

International Mercantile Marine Company, a shipping trust headed by U.S. financier J. Pierpoint Morgan. In 1904 Ismay became President and managing director of I.M.M., and the chairman of Harland and Wolff, William J. Pirrie, became a director of the company. Harland and Wolff, the Belfast shipbuilders, had been building ships for the White Star Line from 1869 onwards. The story of the *Titanic* really begins in 1907 at a dinner party in Pirrie's London mansion in Belgravia. Here Ismay discussed the construction of two huge ships, with a third to be added later. These were to be called Olympic class liners, and they were intended to challenge the government-supported Cunard Line for supremacy on the Atlantic luxury passenger route. The following year a contract letter was signed for construction in the Belfast shipyard of the *Olympic*, the *Titanic* and a third ship, originally to be called the *Gigantic*, but later diplomatically renamed the *Britannic*. The building was to be carried out under the supervision of Lord Pirrie, assisted by his nephew Thomas Andrews. The shipyards were modified to facilitate the construction of these monsters, and a 200-ton floating crane was ordered. As a result the keel was laid down for the *Olympic* (Harland and Wolff number 400) on 16 December 1908, and for the *Titanic* (401) on 31 March 1909.

*Titanic* was described as 'the largest moving object ever made by man', and the facts and figures relating to this ship and her sister are indeed awesome. *Titanic* was 882'9" long, 92'6" wide and 104' high - the equivalent of an eleven-storey building. The centre anchor weighed fifteen-and-a-half tons, and approximately three million rivets were used in her construction. Each of the eight triple expansion engines stood higher than a three-storey building, and steam was provided by 159 furnaces. *Titanic's* elegant design included four funnels, but one of these was a 'dummy', actually used as a ventilation shaft for the engine room. The ship cost £1.5 million, equivalent to £75 million at today's prices, and considerably less than the amount spent on James Cameron's film! Since the finding of the wreck by Dr Robert Ballard in 1985 and subsequent explorations there has been a great deal of speculation about the strength of the steel used in the construction of the ship, but as the ship was being built great

*The Titanic under construction in Harland and Wolff's shipyard in Belfast, 1911*

stress was laid on the need for safety. To ensure this the *Titanic* was built with a double bottom, and the hull was divided into sixteen watertight compartments with fifteen transverse steel bulkheads - any four of these compartments could be breached without causing the ship to sink, and the builders could not envisage such a thing happening.

The *Olympic* was launched on 20 October 1910, and the *Titanic* on 31 May 1911. The White Star Line chartered a steamer *The Duke of Argyll* to bring guests from England to Belfast. 100,000 people were present at the launch, but as was the custom with the Line there was no ceremony involving the breaking of a bottle of champagne. Instead the hull of the ship slid gracefully into the harbour in sixty-two seconds, sliding down the slipway lubricated with twenty-two tons of tallow and soap. Lord Pirrie, Bruce Ismay, Morgan and other guests left on the

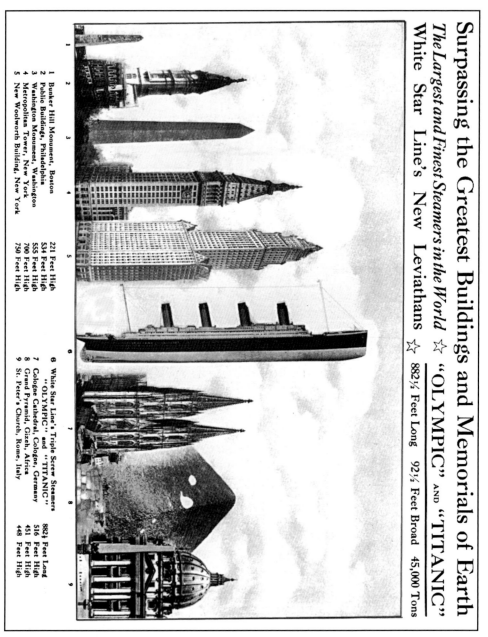

# Surpassing the Greatest Buildings and Memorials of Earth

**The Largest and Finest Steamers in the World** ☆ "OLYMPIC" AND "TITANIC"
White Star Line's New Leviathans ☆ 882½ Feet Long  92½ Feet Broad  45,000 Tons

1  Bunker Hill Monument, Boston                221 Feet High
2  Public Buildings, Philadelphia              534 Feet High
3  Washington Monument, Washington             555 Feet High
4  Metropolitan Tower, New York                700 Feet High
5  New Woolworth Building, New York            750 Feet High

6  White Star Line's Triple Screw Steamers
   "OLYMPIC" and "TITANIC"                    882½ Feet Long
7  Cologne Cathedral, Cologne, Germany         516 Feet High
8  Grand Pyramid, Gizeh, Africa                451 Feet High
9  St. Peter's Church, Rome, Italy             448 Feet High

*White Star advertisement for the Titanic and Olympic comparing their
size with well known landmarks*

14

*The launch of the Titanic on 31 May 1911. Afterwards the distinguished guests adjourned to the Grand Central Hotel in Belfast where they enjoyed Filet de Boeuf and a bottle or two of Chateau Larose 1888 in honour of the occasion*

*Olympic* at 4.30 p.m. The fitting-out of the ship took ten months, three months more than the *Olympic*, and incorporated the features which were to earn the *Titanic* the title of a 'floating palace'. The first-class staterooms, lounge, dining-room and smoking-room were the most luxurious ever built on a liner, and the passenger suites were elaborately furnished in various period designs. Second and third class accommodation was obviously much less luxurious, but it exhibited a far greater degree of comfort than that seen on previous ships. Other impressive features included four passenger elevators, a swimming-pool, a gymnasium with the latest electrical exercise equipment, cigar holders in the first-class bathrooms and an electric potato-peeler in the galley!

The publicity material which was aimed at attracting passengers concentrated on three aspects of the ship: size, splendour and safety. You will notice that this does not include another 's' - speed. The White Star Line made no attempt to challenge the swiftness of the competing Cunarders such as the *Lusitania* and

*The boat deck of the Titanic*

the *Mauretania*. Instead the advertisements depicted *Titanic* and *Olympic* standing upright in a picture which showed that they were 'taller' than any of the world's great buildings. There were colourful pictures of the cabins and public rooms, and comments on the new safety features.

The brochures, however, did not claim that the ships were 'unsinkable' - this was an over-simplification by the press of the safety claims. Despite this publicity, the *Titanic* was far from fully-booked for her maiden voyage from Southampton on 10 April 1912. There were 324 first-class passengers (46% of the capacity), 276 second-class (40%) and 701 third-class or steerage (70%). Some potential customers were obviously concerned about the prospect of sailing on the maiden voyage of such a large and untried ship, but a more obvious reason for the failure to fill the ship was the price of tickets. The average cost of a first-class suite was £300 for the outward crossing only, and this equates to about £15,000 at today's prices. The first-class fare for one

# WHITE STAR LINE.

YOUR ATTENTION IS SPECIALLY DIRECTED TO THE CONDITIONS OF
TRANSPORTATION IN THE ENCLOSED CONTRACT.

THE COMPANY'S LIABILITY FOR BAGGAGE IS STRICTLY LIMITED, BUT
PASSENGERS CAN PROTECT THEMSELVES BY INSURANCE.

*First Class Passenger Ticket per Steamship* Titanic

SAILING FROM Southampton

10/4 1912

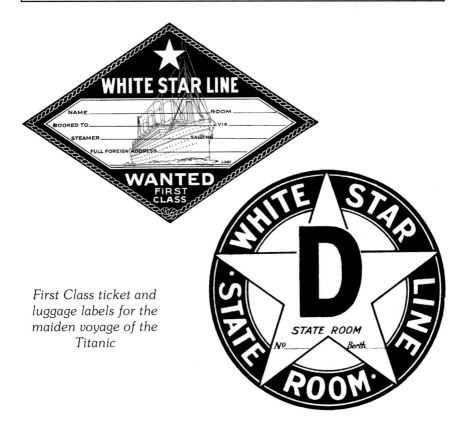

*First Class ticket and
luggage labels for the
maiden voyage of the
Titanic*

person was £30 (£1,500), the second-class £13 (£650) and even the third-class single fare was £8 (£400). When we realise that the skilled craftsmen working on the *Titanic* in Belfast received only £2 per week, and the unskilled £1, the high cost of the fares is obvious.

Despite this, the range of social classes represented by the passengers was enormous. There were twelve millionaires aboard, the wealthiest of whom was the American John Jacob Astor, reputed to be worth £30,000,000; at the other end of the social scale were the steerage passengers, many of them emigrants setting out to make a fresh start in the New World having spent all they owned on their tickets. In fact the 'luxury liner' was officially classed by the Board of Trade as an 'Emigrant Ship', defined as a ship carrying more than fifty steerage passengers (people travelling without cabin accommodation). The regulations for lifeboats issued by the same Board of Trade had failed to keep pace with the size of the new liners, and the requirement for lifeboat capacity was only for 962 persons for a ship licensed to carry 3,547. Thomas Andrews' original designs had provided for sixty-eight lifeboats with capacity for 3,538 persons, but the owners had reduced this number to avoid spoiling the appearance and comfort of the ship. There was, therefore, only room for 1,178 persons - this was to be the principal cause of the great loss of life.

In command of the *Titanic* was 62 year old Captain Edward J. Smith; he was born on 29 January 1850. He was the most experienced of the White Star Commanders, and had been given the task as a tribute to his service and experience. He has been accused of endangering the lives of the passengers by ordering the ship to travel at excessive speed, a charge echoed, as we shall see, by one of the Norfolk survivors. It has also been claimed that he was encouraged in this bid to break the record by J. Bruce Ismay, but it is more likely that Captain Smith's main concern was to get to New York as quickly as possible to ensure that coal stocks lasted. The ship's boilers consumed 650 tons of coal each day, and there had been a shortage of coal in England as a result of a protracted miners' strike. Smith went down with his ship, and there have been many stories told about his last

*Captain Edward J. Smith*

minutes. One problem which he faced was the fact that the crew was only mustered on 6 April, shortly before the ship sailed.

Just before noon on 10 April bells rang out, whistles sounded and tugs led the great liner into the bay at Southampton. Her great size caused so much suction that the steel hawsers of a nearby ship, the *New York*, snapped, causing it to drift into the path of the *Titanic*. Smith ordered a touch ahead on the port engine and the wash pushed the *New York* aside, thereby averting a collision. After this the first part of the voyage went smoothly. At 5.30 p.m. 274 passengers boarded at Cherbourg while twenty-two cross-channel passengers disembarked. The anchor was raised at 8.10 p.m. and the *Titanic* left for Queenstown, Ireland.

Passengers awaiting transfer from Queenstown to the Titanic, lying two miles offshore

By 11.30 a.m. the next day the ship was riding at anchor about two miles from the harbour in Queenstown, the port which has now reverted to its original name of Cobh. 113 third-class and seven second-class passengers boarded from tenders with 1385 bags of mail. Seven passengers disembarked, including Francis Browne, a trainee Jesuit priest from Dublin, who took a series of wonderful photographs of the ship and its passengers. The starboard anchor was raised for the last time at 1.30 p.m., and the ship left for New York, with approximately 2,227 people on board. In calm, clear weather the *Titanic* covered over 905 miles on 12 and 13 April, with the passengers enjoying the comfortable amenities of the ship.

Sunday 14 April was another clear and calm day, but there were a number of ice warnings received from other ships. Some were passed to the Captain, but at other times the wireless operators, Harold Bride and John Phillips, were too busy to pay much attention to them. The operators were employed by Marconi, and their main duty was to make money by relaying personal messages from the passengers. The wireless had broken down two days earlier, so there was a backlog to deal with, especially as they were now within range of Cape Race, the receiving station. At 11.40 p.m. the lookouts in the crow's nest, Frederick Fleet and Reginald Lee saw an iceberg dead ahead about 500 yards away towering some sixty feet above the water. The fact that they did not see the iceberg earlier can be attributed to two main causes: the calmness of the water meant that the sea was not lapping against the berg, and the lookouts had not been issued with the correct night binoculars. As it was, from one point of view they saw it too quickly - had they not given a warning to the bridge the *Titanic* might have collided head-on, doing structural damage which would not have proved fatal. As it was, their warning enabled First Officer William Murdoch to order 'hard-a-starboard' to the helmsman and then 'stop engines' to the engine room. It is possible that Murdoch had also seen the iceberg as the ship approached it. After several seconds the giant liner veered to port, but the iceberg struck the starboard bow side, brushed along the side of the ship and passed on. The impact was slight, and was not noticed by many of the passengers.

It has been thought for a long time that the impact caused a narrow gash running 300 feet along the side, but research carried out since the discovery of the wreck in 1985 has suggested other theories: the weak steel splitting, the rivets popping, and, more recently, the idea that there was a series of small pin-pricks rather than a long gash. What we do know for certain is that five of the compartments began to take on water, and that by 11.50 p.m. boiler room six was flooded in eight feet of water. Andrews inspected the ship, informed Captain Smith that it was doomed, and calculated that it would stay afloat for one to one-and-a-half hours only. In fact the *Titanic* stayed afloat for two hours, forty minutes - a tribute to the designers and to those manning the pumps.

This should have allowed ample time for all on board to find places in the lifeboats, but Smith and Andrews knew that there was room for only about half the passengers and crew. Nevertheless, orders were given to uncover the lifeboats and muster the crew and passengers. Phillips and Bride began sending distress signals, using first of all the call sign CQD and later the recently-introduced message SOS. Numerous ships heard the message, including the *Carpathia* fifty-eight miles away. Unfortunately the ship generally reckoned to be nearest to the *Titanic*, the *Californian*, did not respond - its operator had switched off at 11.30 p.m. as was his custom. As there had been no boat-drill the loading of the lifeboats was badly organised, resulting in a failure to fill them properly; the first boat to be lowered, Starboard number 7 was capable of carrying sixty-five people but it left with only twenty-eight on board.

Much of what happened in the next two hours has been the stuff of history and legend. We know that there was panic, and that shots were fired into the air to prevent an already full boat being swamped. There were scenes of cowardice, with men trying to evade the order 'Women and Children First'. We know, too, that there were scenes of heroism, as exemplified by the deaths of Ida and Isidor Straus, whose story is told in another chapter of this book. All the engineers on board died, as did the members of the orchestra under their leader Wallace Hartley. Survivors have disputed the exact title of the last piece of music they played,

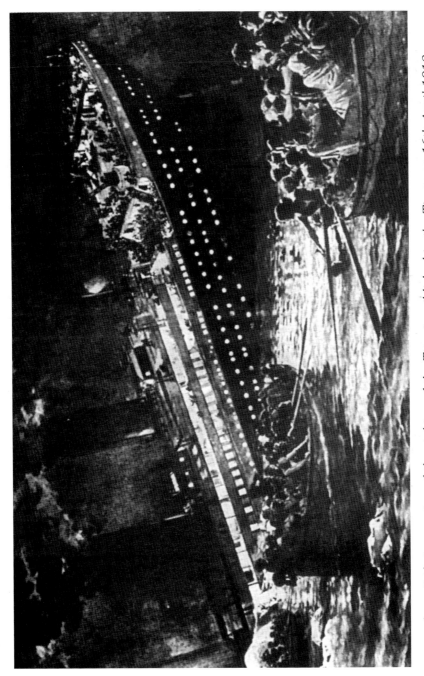

*An artist's impression of the sinking of the Titanic published in the Times on 16th April 1912*

*The Carpathia*

although strong support for the idea that it was the hymn 'Nearer My God To Thee' came from one of the most vocal of those who were rescued, Eva Hart. Shortly after 2.15 a.m. the forward funnel collapsed, and Captain Smith released the crew members from their duties with the words 'It's every man for himself'. The ship broke in two, a fact not verified until 1985, and the stern section righted itself for a few moments in the water before slowly sinking into the sea. Over 1,520 had been lost, and 705 had survived. Eighty-one per cent of the men had drowned, twenty-three per cent of the women, and about half the one hundred children on board - almost all the children who were lost were in third-class. In all, sixty-three per cent of the first-class passengers had survived, forty-two per cent of the second-class, twenty-five per cent of the third-class and twenty-three per cent of the crew. The two halves of the *Titanic* sank to the bed of the Atlantic, two-and-a-half miles below.

At 3.30 a.m. the rockets of the *Carpathia* were sighted by the survivors in the lifeboats. She had raced to the rescue at $17\frac{1}{2}$ knots although her normal speed was $14\frac{1}{2}$ knots. By 8.30 a.m. all the survivors had been picked up, the adults climbing up swaying rope-ladders, and the children placed in sacks and hauled aboard in luggage-nets. The last survivor to climb on to the *Carpathia* was Second Officer Charles Lightoller.

The ship reached New York at 9.00 p.m. on 18 April, and four days later the Inquiry headed by Senator William A. Smith began. Eighty-two witnesses were called. The report gave factual details first, and then condemned Captain Lord of the *Californian* for failing to respond to the *Titanic's* distress signals. It recommended a number of safety improvements which included new lifeboat regulations, twenty-four hour radio watches, and a clearing up of the muddle concerning signals. These recommendations were adopted, and together with other

*Lifeboats approaching the Carpathia*

*Second Officer Charles Lightoller as a young*
*merchant marine officer*

measures such as the setting-up of a North Atlantic Ice Patrol they have helped to increase safety for those making the journey - one positive outcome of the tragedy. Smith's report was accepted by the Senate and hailed by the American press, but in England he was attacked for attempting to blame the whole disaster on the British. His inquiry overlapped the one set up in Britain under the Wreck Commissioner, Lord Mersey, which was held in an unsuitable Drill Hall at Buckingham Gate, London. The assessors toured the *Olympic* and questioned one hundred witnesses including Ismay, Marconi, the captain of the *Carpathia* and Sir Ernest Shackleton the explorer and an expert on icebergs. They heard directly from only two passengers, from first class, the Duff Gordons, who insisted upon testifying. The Inquiry was at pains to avoid damaging the British shipping interests, and although it identified a number of human errors which were responsible for the tragedy, no one was punished. Lightoller described the findings as using 'the whitewash brush'.

Shortly after the *Titanic* sank the White Star Line chartered four vessels which recovered 328 bodies with 209 being returned to Halifax, Nova Scotia; the badly damaged or deteriorated bodies were buried at sea. Of the 119 buried at sea, about 60 were identified at the time and 49 remain unidentified. Some bodies, including John Jacob Astor, were claimed by relatives, and the remaining 150 victims were buried in ceremonies from May 3 to June 12, 1912 in three Halifax cemeteries. Nineteen are in the Mount Olivet Catholic Cemetery, ten are in the Baron de Hirsch Jewish Cemetery, and 121 are in the Fairview Lawn Cemetery. Of these, 42 remain unidentified.

*Fairview Lawn Cemetery, Halifax, Nova Scotia*

As we shall see from the reaction in Norfolk there was tremendous public interest and a great deal of practical sympathy in the immediate aftermath of the disaster. Soon, however, more important events were to occupy the minds of politicians and ordinary people alike, as the events leading up to the First World War began to dominate the headlines. Many survivors were

*Mount Olivet Catholic Cemetery, Halifax, Nova Scotia*

reluctant to talk about the tragedy. As early as 1912 a feature film about the *Titanic* was made, but the first full-length film *Atlantic* did not appear until 1929. Twentieth-Century Fox produced a film called *Titanic* (original title *Nearer My God To Thee*) in 1953, but it was not until three years later that a new upsurge in interest was created, first by the publication of Walter Lord's book *A Night To Remember*, and then by the film of the same name which was premiered at the Odeon, Leicester Square, on 3 July 1958. It starred Kenneth More as Lightoller and, despite its limited budget, gave a largely authentic and very moving account of the events of April 1912. Notable for other reasons was the 1980 film *Raise The Titanic* which combined an improbable plot with the equally improbable (but extremely impressive) sight of an unscathed *Titanic* rising majestically from the ocean. Its main claim to fame was its cost which led Lew Grade to make the celebrated comment that instead of raising the *Titanic* it would have been cheaper to sink the Atlantic!

There have always been dedicated enthusiasts who are obsessed with this story, but the next event which rekindled the interest of the general public was the finding of the wreck in

1985. Earlier attempts to locate the ship had failed, but on 1 September 1985 Dr Robert Ballard led a joint French-American expedition from Woods Hole Oceanographic Institute, Massachusetts, and the French IFREMER Institute, which discovered the wreckage site at a depth of 12,460 feet on the ocean floor. Pictures were taken by remote control only, until July 1986 when Ballard and his American colleagues returned to the wreck in the submersible *Alvin* and took close-up pictures with the aid of a robot camera *JJ* (Jason Junior). Ballard decided to leave all the debris on the sea bed, adding only a memorial plaque. The following year the U.S. Congress attempted to make the *Titanic*, lying in international waters, an international memorial, but August of that year IFREMER (now no longer with Ballard) and RMS Titanic Inc. of New York brought up a large number of artefacts at a cost of four million pounds. This, and subsequent retrieval expeditions, caused great controversy as many (including some survivors and their relatives) regard the site as a grave. The latest venture has been the raising of a piece of the hull in August 1998.

A number of the artefacts were put on display at a highly successful exhibition at Greenwich, and its popularity showed how great has been the interest in the *Titanic* in the 1990s. There is a constant stream of books, videos, models, stamps, jigsaws and replicas, and an ever-increasing torrent of theories to account for what happened. Time has dimmed some of the memories, and there are now (in 1999) only five survivors left world-wide. The success of the James Cameron film has given added impetus to a tide of interest which was already growing. The sheer scale of the tragedy, the controversies which still rage, the mysteries which will never be solved, above all the human impact of the story - these will ensure *Titanic's* place as the most famous shipwreck in history.

# Chapter Two

# The Norfolk Survivors -
# Frank Prentice

## 'Almost like murder ...'

One of the most interesting aspects of the *Titanic* story is the way in which the tragedy brought together the rich and famous on the one hand and ordinary people on the other, all faced with the same desperate predicament; millionaires and steerage passengers perished at the same time, and important and unknown passengers found themselves in the same lifeboat. This fascinating scenario is well illustrated by the stories of the five people from the county of Norfolk who survived that night, each of them linked in some way with others who have played a much more prominent part in the *Titanic* story.

The events surrounding the survival of Frank Prentice have become part of *Titanic* legend as a result of the publicity given to Mrs Virginia Clark from Los Angeles. Frank helped the wealthy Los Angeles socialite to put on her lifebelt, assuring her, 'It's just a precaution.' She allowed herself to be placed in Lifeboat 4, together with Mrs John Jacob Astor and her maid, and watched the ship sink at 2.20 a.m. After Quartermaster Walter Perkis insisted that the lifeboat should return to help some of the swimmers in the water, Virginia recognised one of the five men who were pulled from the water - it was Frank Prentice. She wrapped her coat around him and began rubbing his limbs to try to revive him; he survived while two of the others died of exposure.

Frank's great-great niece, Sue Roberson, confirms that his second name was Winnold, not George as appears in a number of reports on the crew members. His mother and father kept the Castle Hotel in Downham Market, West Norfolk, and Frank was born there on the 17 February 1896. By 1912 he was living in

*Frank Prentice as a young man, shortly before joining the Titanic*

Denzil Avenue, Southampton, and he was available to sign on as a storekeeper aboard the *Titanic* in April. He had been ordered to report from Liverpool where he was about to set sail on the *Adriatic*. This was typical of many of the crew who joined the *Titanic* just before the start of the maiden voyage. In newspaper and radio interviews given just before he died in May 1982 he commented that, as one of the youngest members of the crew at 16, he was 'general dogsbody to the purser. My job was looking after sea-pay rolls, cargo and passenger manifests.' He described the atmosphere on board as, 'one merry party - the best of food, the best of dinner, orchestras, dancing. She was a fine ship, absolutely super, carrying the cream of passengers in her.'

He felt that the ship was travelling too quickly, and was on the course which was too northerly, 'We should have been about three hundred miles away from the ice, but we were out to break a record, and if ever a ship was thrown away, *Titanic*, the beautiful ship was thrown away. If we had not hit that one we would have hit something else. That was the tragedy - speed.'

He was in his cabin with six others from the purser's department when the ship glided to a halt and stopped. He said, 'There was no moon, the sea was dead calm. I had no idea when I went on deck that she had ripped herself so badly ... there were people walking around, nobody knew what had happened. She was gradually listing over to port, and we had orders to get the boats out ... the distance from the lifeboats to the water was seventy odd feet. There was no panic, and we started to get women and children into the boats. She was listing all the time. I heard Andrews, the designer, tell Bruce Ismay and Captain Smith that the ship was going to sink. There were people then rushing around, and I went down to the storeroom with a gang of men and we collected all the biscuits, but we couldn't get near the boats as it was a bit of a shambles by then. I came across a young couple and she was having trouble with her lifebelt, but we persuaded her to get into the lifeboat.

The weather was wonderful, but it was absolutely freezing - ice everywhere. I put my lifebelt on, but by then all the boats had been got away, so there was chaos. I couldn't do any more, so I decided to go up aft ... it was very quiet up there, and whilst I

*Frank Prentice in 1982, shortly before his death*

was up there they sent up eight rockets from the bridge, and we could see our lifeboats stretched out … there were no boats near us at all. Whilst we were up there she gradually sank by the head, and you could feel everything going through her … she went down and then she came up so she was almost vertical out of the water.' He thought it unlikely that he would survive, but he, 'said a few prayers and jumped. As I passed I saw the two propeller blades looming out of the ship's side. I hit the water with a terrific bang which knocked all the wind out of me … the wreckage was all round the stern, and there were nearly a hundred people around the stern, too. I stayed down there amongst all these people. There was somebody shouting, "Stay together, we have more chance of being picked up if we stay together." And all those wailings and sobbings and praying … all the noises died away because the *Titanic* had glided away very quietly. I thought I was all alone as there were no sounds coming, but then I realised that I had seen where the lifeboats were. I picked up another lifebelt and tucked it under myself, and then a cushion; I paddled away, although I was gradually feeling that I was freezing up. My feet were in a very bad way ... I had boots on and they were hurting me a bit. Eventually I saw a lifeboat and they picked me up. I sat in next to a woman there, and this was Mrs Clark whose lifebelt I had put on; there was a fireman dead in the bottom of the boat ... the boat had about a foot of water in. There were only two other men on board the lifeboat. Mrs Clark wrapped her coat around me and I think she saved my life - I probably saved her life and then she saved mine! That was rather a coincidence, wasn't it?'

According to Marshall Everett, Frank was one of the last men off the *Titanic* to reach the *Carpathia*. Unable to walk, he was slung aboard in a basket. He recovered quickly, however, and returned to Britain on the *Lapland*. In his final comments to a newspaper reporter, Peter Williams, Frank Prentice blamed Captain Smith and the White Star Line for irresponsibility. 'We were going far too quickly through the ice. And if only there'd been enough lifeboats, no one need have died. It was almost like murder, wasn't it?' Frank repeated this assertion in an ITV documentary when at the age of 87 he remembered the events of that night, 71 years before. Shortly afterwards he died on 19 May 1982.

# Chapter Three

# The Norfolk Survivors -
# Ellen Bird

## *'The rescue of an Old Buckenham Girl'*

In Lifeboat 8 was a survivor who epitomises the juxtaposition of the ordinary and the rich and famous in the *Titanic* story. Ellen Bird was the daughter of a humble shepherd who lived in a small village in rural Norfolk - indeed the family did not even live in the village of Old Buckenham but on the outskirts, in a small group of cottages which formed the hamlet of Staxford. Even today this is an isolated spot, but with the help of a local resident, Thora Lindenmayer, I located the small group of cottages which contained the Old Bird Cage, the birthplace of Ellen. She was one of eleven children born to Maryann and Samuel (always known as Shepherd) Bird. Her mother was 39 and her father 40 when Ellen was born in 1881, on 8 April. Her elder brothers were George, Samuel and Benjamin, and she had five older sisters, Sarah, Emma, Anna, Eliza and Mary. Two other children were born after Ellen - Abigail in 1883 and William in 1885.

The next we hear of Ellen is when she became the maid of Ida Straus, wife of the millionaire owner of Macy's Department Store, New York. Evidence from the Straus Family Historical Society suggests that Mr and Mrs Straus had been in Europe since January 1912, and that they had tried unsuccessfully to hire a French maid. They then employed an English maid prior to sailing, but when she left them Ellen was employed, with Ida writing to her children to express the hope that the new maid would 'work out'.

As part of Ticket 17483, Ellen boarded the ship at Southampton, going about her duties until Sunday, 14 April. She travelled in Cabin C.97.

*Ida and Isidor Straus*

The heroism of Isidor and Ida Straus is a well-documented part of the story of the loading of the lifeboats. Ida and Isidor were Jewish emigrants to the United States who had been married for 38 years. They were generous supporters of many charities and Isidor had served in the Congress of the United States. They continued to serve others despite the anti-Semitism they faced in New York, and they were devoted to each other and to their seven children. Ironically, Isidor had written a letter in 1904 to, 'As good a wife as ever man was blessed with' ... giving her advice 'in case I should die before you.' She died with him on 15 April, 1912, and her refusal to leave him, and his refusal to take the place of a younger person in a boat have captured the imagination of all who are interested in the sinking. Memorial services for them were held all over New York, and one was attended by 40,000 people. The employees of Macy's Department Store paid for a plaque in their memory to be placed over the 135 West 34th Street entrance, still known as the Memorial Entrance. Isidor's body was recovered from the sea on 1 May 1912, and buried in New York, but that of Ida, his beloved wife, was never found.

In this well-remembered heroic story Ellen Bird plays her part. One account gives the following information, 'At first Mrs Straus seemed uncertain what to do. At one point she handed some small jewellery to her maid, Ellen Bird, then took it back again. Later she crossed the Boat Deck and almost entered Lifeboat 8 - then turned around and rejoined Mr Straus. Now her mind was made up, 'We have been living together for many years. Where you go, I go.' Archibald Gracie, Hugh Woolmer and other friends tried in vain to make her go ... Ida and Isidor sat down together on a pile of deck chairs.' In 1985, after Robert Ballard's discovery of the wreck, Iphigene Sulzberger, an elderly daughter of Adolph Ochs, the founder of the *New York Times*, wrote a brief article in the paper in which she described how Mrs Straus, before Ellen got into a lifeboat, had taken off her fur coat and said, 'Wear this, it will be cold in the lifeboat, and I do not need it any more.' When the *Carpathia* reached New York, Ellen took the coat to Sara Straus, Mrs Straus's eldest daughter, but was told to keep it as it was her mother's gift to her. It is possible that in New

*Staxford, where Ellen Bird was born*

York Ellen contacted the Spedden family - she may well have helped to look after young Robert Douglas Spedden, aged six, on the *Carpathia*.

Back home in England, a local Norfolk paper, the *Eastern Evening News*, reported on Monday, 22 April that 'Mr and Mrs S. Bird, of Old Buckenham, were delighted on Saturday when receiving news of the safety of their daughter who was a passenger on the *Titanic*. Miss Bird only a few weeks ago entered the service of Mrs Isidor Straus, and was accompanying that lady to New York. Although Mrs Straus's heroic death with her husband had been announced, the fate of her maid was not certain. The receipt of the good news by her parents came as a great relief after the suspense they had endured for several days.' A sister paper, the *Eastern Daily Press* had this report on Wednesday, 12 May:

'THE RESCUE OF AN OLD BUCKENHAM GIRL'

'The rescue of Miss Bird was described by one of the witnesses at the Washington enquiry. Alfred Crawford, steward, stated that when the *Titanic* struck the iceberg he went below and told his passengers to dress warmly, after which he conducted them to

*Old Buckenham Church and the school Ellen Bird attended*

39

the Boat Deck. Mrs Straus placed her maid in Boat 8, and was about to get in herself when suddenly she turned and flung her arms around her husband's neck, saying, "We've been all these years together. Wherever you go I go" and refused to get in.'

An interesting postcard, with a picture of the *Titanic* on the reverse, was sent by Ellen to her niece, Evelyn Dewhurst (nee Symonds). This is signed Auntie E. although she was usually referred to as Nellie by the family. The text reads 'I send you my love and heartiest congratulations. I am glad your plant won the 2nd prize and I am also glad your Dad won some prizes. Your loving Auntie E.'

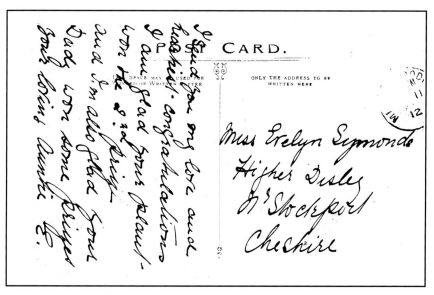

*The Titanic postcard sent by Ellen Bird*

There is only sketchy information about what happened to Ellen after this. She settled in America, married a yacht captain called Edward Beattie, and continued to work for various wealthy families. She died, childless, in a convalescent home in Newport, Rhode Island, on 11 September 1949, aged 68, and was buried in Acushnet Cemetery, Massachusetts. Her brother, William, informed the authorities of her death, which was the result of cerebral thrombosis.

# Chapter Four

# The Norfolk Survivors - The Beanes

## *'We were saved together'*

In the Broadway musical which opened in April 1997, one of the passengers on the *Titanic* is a loud-mouthed American social climber called Alice Beane who does a running commentary on the media superstars in first class. The name of Mrs Beane has been plucked at random from the passenger list by the show's writer, but the character as presented here is a far cry from the real Mrs Beane, a second-class English passenger from Norwich, Norfolk. Ethel and her husband Edward represent one of the few happy-endings in stories involving newly-weds aboard the *Titanic* - in most cases the husband died while the wife survived.

Ethel Clarke was 19 years old when she married Ted Beane in 1912; their fathers both worked at Bullard's Brewery in Norwich, and Ethel herself was a barmaid in a public-house on Dereham Road named the Lord Nelson, after Norfolk's most famous sea-faring son (it is now completely refurbished and called Dodgers). Ted, who was in the building trade, was 32 when they married and for some time had worked for half the year in America and half the year in England. When they married he made plans to take his young bride, aged 19, to America and, although he normally travelled third class, he booked them second-class berths on the *Titanic* - this may well have saved their lives. As the ship was sinking he pushed Ethel into Lifeboat 13 then dived overboard, and swam in the icy sea until he was clear of the vessel and could be picked up. Family tradition, as reported to me by Edward (John) Clarke, son of Ethel's youngest brother, has always maintained that Ethel pulled a swimmer from the sea into her lifeboat, only to find that she had saved her husband.

*Ted and Ethel Beane with their children George and Edward*

This was certainly the account given on the 1 May 1912 in the local paper the *Eastern Daily Press* which had earlier reported on Saturday, 20 April that, 'Mrs G. Clarke, of 33 Bond Street, Norwich, last evening received the following telegram from her daughter, Mrs Beane. "Both arrived safely, Carpathia. Will write. Ethel. New York".' On Wednesday 1 May with the headline 'News of Norfolk Survivors. How Mr and Mrs Beane Were Saved', the paper quoted from the *New York Times*, 'Beane stood back at the cry of "No, only women" when his bride was placed in one of the lifeboats. But as he stood back manfully, he saw the boat pull off, and that it was only half full. And he jumped into the sea, and swam for that boat, and Ethel Beane's arms pulled him in.'

The *Eastern Daily Press* echoed the despair of many of the passengers when it reported that 'all that the Beanes had in the world went down with the ship, and they had saved six years for the wedding which took place in Norwich six weeks ago. Between them they had stored away £100, and sixty-five wedding presents were lost with the money'. Ethel had written to her father from on board the *Carpathia*, and the words of this very ordinary Norwich girl are an eloquent testimony to the personal sadness of the tragedy, 'Thank God we are both saved together. There are 150 widows on this boat ... I have not got even a hair pin to call my own. But we must be thankful we were saved together, as they were shooting down the men who came into the ladies' boats. We were not far from the liner when it went down, and the screaming and the shouting were dreadful. We were rescued at five o'clock in the morning and hauled up by ladders and big ropes, as none of us could feel ourselves. We were put in hot rooms, with blankets, and had plenty of brandy, but a great many have died since they were rescued.'

Edward and Ethel settled in America, raised a family, and remained there. In an article in the *Eastern Evening News* on Tuesday, 17 April 1973, sixty-one years after the tragedy, *Whiffler* recorded an interview with Ted Hardiment of Colman Road, Norwich, Ethel's brother-in-law. At this time she was still alive, an old lady of nearly 80, and Ted reported that she still had fear of water, instilled in her on that night in April 1912. 'It was her first and last journey across the Atlantic', he said. 'I don't think she would fly over, and I am certain she would not come over on a ship.' Ethel Clarke was the sister of Ted's wife, Ida, and also of Charles Clarke. Mr Hardiment recalls his mother-in-law describing how they waited in suspense for news of the survivors. 'They lived at the newspaper office until news came through.' Another local newspaper, the *Norwich Mercury*, had reported on April 17th, 'It is needless to say that news of whether this unfortunate couple are among the saved is being awaited with painful interest.' Edward and Ethel brought up their two sons, George and Edward Junior, in New York, and lived there until their deaths - Edward's in 1968 at the age of 88, and Ethel in 1992 in her 90th year. In 1985, the year of the discovery of the wreck of the *Titanic*, a local journalist, James Ruddy, wrote about the couple under the headline 'They Lived to Tell the Tale.' 'Young love. Tragedy. Suspense … it is the kind of tale which would make Barbara Cartland and movie moguls drool with satisfaction'. Of course, he could not foresee James Cameron, Kate Winslet and Leonardo di Caprio!

# Chapter Five

# The Norfolk Survivors -
# May Howard

## *'Arrived Safe'*

With the fifth and last Norfolk survivor we come to the most startling example of the fact that the famous and the humble found themselves side by side on that night. In Collapsible C, the last starboard-side boat to be launched, we find J. Bruce Ismay, whose importance and, to many, infamy are well documented in *Titanic* literature, and May Howard, a domestic servant from a small market town, North Walsham. The contrast could hardly be greater! J. Bruce Ismay was the Managing Director of the White Star Line and in many ways the most influential passenger on the ship. He has been accused of putting pressure on Captain E. J. Smith to increase speed, thus contributing to the disaster. This would have been enough to make him the villain of the piece in many people's eyes, but his reputation suffered even more because he survived. The *Titanic* sank on his 50th birthday, and he was attacked in the press as 'J. Brute Ismay'. The *New York American* suggested, as a comment on Ismay, 'that the emblem of the White Star Line be changed from a white star to a white liver'. There are conflicting stories about his survival, ranging from a report that he was picked up and dumped into a lifeboat by Chief Officer Henry Wilde to the claim that he ordered a boat for himself to be manned by experienced oarsmen. His own claim was that as there were no women and children passengers around he stepped into what he thought was the last lifeboat. His haunted look as he watches the sinking of the ship is one of the most enduring images of the fine 1958 film *A Night To Remember*. Whatever happened the fact that he was saved, and that he was so evasive at subsequent enquiries, created

*May Howard*

a scandal from which Ismay never escaped. What a contrast to a young Norfolk girl going out to join her brothers in Toronto.

The local newspapers in Norfolk reported on Friday 19 April that 'an additional list of survivors published this morning contains the name of Mary (sic) Howard. This is the name of the young woman who was going out from North Walsham'. Further details were provided on 2 May under the headline 'Norfolk Girl on the *Titanic* - How May Howard Was Saved' "Extracts from a Toronto newspaper whose correspondent interviewed Miss Howard in New York. This is her story; 'I was in my berth (3rd class) about midnight on Sunday, when there came a rocking of the boat that tossed us about a bit. Then came a terrible ringing of bells, followed in a little while by the doctor, who came down and said everything was all right, but we had better get our life belts. The foreigners behaved badly. Then they let us come right up to the deck where the boats were, and then I saw they were getting people into the boats. The women were not terrified, as they all thought that they would see their husbands again. The officers behaved splendidly, as well as the men, and the people were put into the boats without any trouble ... we rowed away a little. Then we saw the lights in the ship going down, and I am sure she broke in two, and one part seemed to float away and sway before sinking. We couldn't see people on the decks because it was too dark, and we were a good bit away from her when we last saw her. When the light came there was the *Carpathia* and another steamer. We could read her name - *Californian* ... I lost my box, my money and everything'. Though she tells the story simply (adds the correspondent) there is plenty of evidence that the shock is greater than she realises yet."

This was the only information we had concerning May until November 1996, when a request from a local journalist, Chris Stokes, revealed the fact that May's niece, Gladys Whitwood, was living in North Walsham. Gladys has provided us with information, much of it from her mother Emily, May's sister, with photographs of May, and with the telegram (now in pieces) sent by her from Western Union, New York, which reads 'Arrived safe will write. May'. May was one of six children, and had decided to join her brothers who had already emigrated to Canada. She

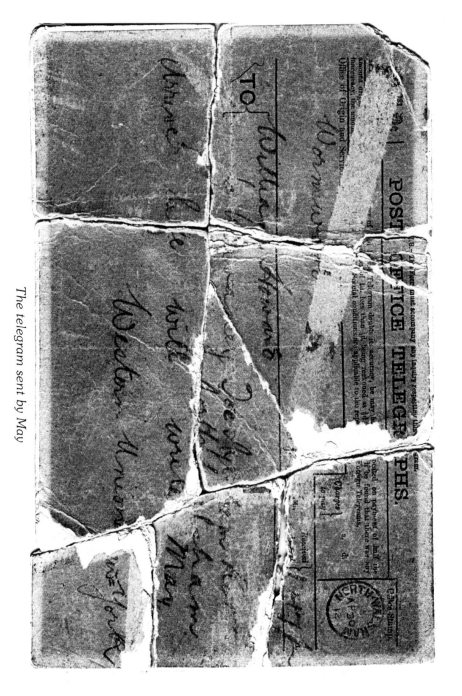

The telegram sent by May

48

*May's niece, Gladys Whitworth, with bouquet, judging a school's
drawing competition in North Walsham*

hoped to become a nanny near their home in Toronto, and they
had offered to pay her fare. Although the report in the Toronto
paper reported that she had lost everything, Gladys told us that
May had saved one of her treasures - a brooch with the inscription
'Faith, Hope, Charity', a gift from Gladys's father. May went
from New York to Toronto, joined her brothers and became a
nanny. Gladys completes the story, 'She never married, she never
returned to England, and I'm not sure when she died, but she
certainly achieved what she set out to do.'

NO. 172

WITH TONIC SOL-FA.

This Song may be Sung in Public without Fee or License except at Theatres or Music Halls.

# THE SHIP THAT WILL NEVER RETURN

## *(The Loss of the "Titanic.")*

SONG

AND

POEM

Written & Composed

by

# F. V. S⊤· CLAIR.

LONDON.

E. MARKS & SON

125, MARE STREET, HACKNEY, N.E.

AND 35 ROSOMAN STREET E.C.

COPYRIGHT.

ENT. STA. HALL.

50

One of the popular songs composed after the sinking, *The Ship That Will Never Return*, by F. V. St Clair, finishes with these lines:

*'When rich men and poor men went down side by side*
*Where Rank made no difference for Death levelled all.'*

This sentiment is certainly not shown to be true if the comparative figures for percentages saved from 1st and 3rd class are compared, but it does have a strange kind of truth in the fact that the tragedy did bring together the famous and the unknown, the influential and the unimportant in the scenes which took place on the *Titanic* and in the lifeboats as she went down. Certainly the stories of the five Norfolk survivors are proof of the fact that much of the interest in what happened lies in what we can discover about the ordinary people whose lives were changed by that 'night to remember'.

# Chapter Six

# Reports and Comments in the Local Press

## 'Read all about it ...'

In his book *The Titanic Disaster - As Reported in the British National Press*, Dave Bryceson comments that 'living as we do now in an age of rapidly progressing technology it is hard for us to imagine a time when there were no radio or television services ... in 1912 the only two methods by which news was spread were by word of mouth and the daily newspapers.' He points out that by Tuesday 16 April the headlines were shaking the whole of Britain and indeed the world. On the previous day, however, confused and false information had presented a much more optimistic picture. The *New York Times* had broken the news of the sinking on 15 April (on the same day the paper was still carrying an advertisement for the liner's return voyage to England!), but later that same morning a wireless message was received saying that the *Titanic* was being towed into Halifax by the steamer *Virginian*, and that everyone on board was safe. The White Star office began to make preparations to receive the passengers and to transfer them to New York, and the *Times* was criticised for running such a pessimistic story that morning. It later emerged that the false news that all were safe was the result of two garbled messages which had been linked together. Hungry for news and in a desire to think positively, the papers had made incorrect assumptions about what had happened. This resulted in banner headlines such as that in the *New York Sun* - ALL SAVED FROM TITANIC AFTER COLLISION. The first authentic news was received in Wanamaker's Department Store

*A typical newsvendor's billboard on the afternoon of 15 April 1912*

in New York on their powerful radio equipment at 4.35 p.m.; the *Titanic's* sister ship, the *Olympic* reported from the scene of the disaster 1,400 miles away that the ship had gone down, and the *Carpathia* was steaming to New York with about 675 survivors.

The early ill-founded and ironic optimism was echoed in the confusion shown by the local papers in Norfolk. These were the headlines and this was the report in the *Eastern Evening News* on Monday 15 April:

DISASTER TO GREAT LINER

TITANIC COLLIDES WITH ICEBERG

WIRELESS APPEAL FOR HELP

ALL PASSENGERS TAKEN OFF

ILL-FATED MAIDEN VOYAGE

'Reuters states that Liner *Virginian* reports wireless communication that *Titanic* in collision with iceberg - requested assistance - *Virginian* hastening to her aid.'

**NORWICH.**

**ALUE!**

**32/6.**

edsteads, from 15/6.

alities and of the
ys kept in stock.

-date hygienic principles.

**EANING.**

ON TO
E OF

ns, Mats and
ts, Varnishes,

rkets for
ustomers

PRICES WHICH DEFY
EFUL COMPETITION.

**EY**, WALL PAPER
FACTORS ::

treets, Norwich.

and at YARMOUTH.

**DILEMMA**

ION.

W SPRING SUIT?

**TION**

**SON'S**

TAILOR.

latest Bannockburn
teads, Blue Serges,
New Greys

THE MERITS OF

**RVISION.**

VALUE.

---

## Eastern Evening News

NORWICH, FRIDAY, APRIL 19, 1912.

The arrangements for the sale of coal at reasonable prices to certain selected classes of poor people in Norwich during the coal strike have worked admirably. They have enabled a very large number of people whose means are so small that the unnecessary expenditure of a penny is a hardship to them to secure a supply of coal at normal prices, and have saved the very poorest people in the city from the fuel famine which they would otherwise have had to face. The strike is now over, and coal prices are falling towards a normal point again; and, the need for the special arrangements being over, they will be discontinued and no further tickets issued after the end of this week. The very hearty thanks of the poor of the city are due to the Lord Mayor for the wise and practical step taken to meet an emergency which every one will agree in hoping will never occur again.

The half-yearly report presented to Thursday's meeting of the Eastern Sea Fisheries Committee is not nearly so favourable as could be wished. In certain minor departments of the shell fish industry good quantities and of good quality have been obtained; but on the whole the longshore fishermen who work from the possession of fishing villages round the North Norfolk coast have not had the best of luck. The sprat fishing was again a failure; so much so that the experience of the few crews who tried it was sufficient to cause others to leave it alone. The weather in October alone, so far as the crab fishing, it was brought to a sudden finish by the gale at the end of September, in which a great loss of crab traps occurred, the Sheringham men being especially heavy sufferers, their loss amounting to eight hundred traps. Altogether it was not a good season; but our longshore fishermen are so accustomed to take the rough with the smooth, and like all men whose dealings are with the sea have learned the large patience that comes of life spent in that way. We hope for better things for them when the next report is presented.

An exceedingly interesting section of the report is that which deals with the research work carried out during the season with regard to the migration of edible crabs. A large number of edible crabs were liberated along the Norfolk and Lincolnshire coasts, with numbered brass labels attached to them, and up to the present about 23 per cent. of them have been recaptured. Beyond proving the fact that 73 miles is the maximum distance any one of them was found to have travelled, the report does not give many particulars, for which possibly we may have to wait till a larger percentage have been recaptured and figures covering a wider series can be collated. But one fact which is reported raises a very interesting question indeed. Two crabs, we are told, liberated at different places, were recaptured in the same trap in the neighbourhood of their old home on the Yorkshire coast. Have crabs then a homing instinct? Such an inference would seem to something of the kind. That jun...

---

# FULL STORIES BY TITANIC'S SURVIVORS

## HOW THE LINER WENT DOWN

## EXPLOSIONS AFTER CRASH

## BAND PLAYING "NEARER MY GOD"

## REPORTED SUICIDE OF THE CAPTAIN

## HEARTRENDING SCENES AND AMAZING ESCAPES

## HOW THE BOATS WERE FILLED

The full stories of the survivors of the Titanic are now to hand, and describe heartrending scenes and amazing escapes.

The great liner went down with the band playing "Nearer, my God, to Thee," taking all but 745 of her human cargo of 2340.

The Titanic was ripped from stern to stern by a gigantic mass of ice, which tore her along the side as though by a huge can-opener.

For two minutes, it is said, 150 feet of her stern were poised above the sea line, before with a slanting dive she disappeared in the waters. Hundreds were grouped upon her decks, and their cries were heart-rending.

**REUTER'S TELEGRAMS.**

NEW YORK, April 18, 9.5 p.m.

The Carpathia arrived at the pier at 8.37. Five hundred friends and relatives were enabled in the pier shortly after. Mr. J. P. Morgan, jun., appeared on the scene as the boat was about to dock, also representatives of the Widener and Thayer families, who arrived by special trains from Philadelphia. There were one thousand people in the dock's ten minutes later, and many weeping outside. Motor cars kept rushing up, bringing fresh arrivals.

9.30 p.m.

The Committee of the New York Stock Exchange brought to the pier shortly before the Carpathia arrived a sum of 20,000 dollars to be distributed among those on board most in need of assistance. Several Red Cross nurses and a dozen physicians arrived on the scene.

LANDING OF SURVIVORS.

10 p.m.

The first survivors began to leave the ship at twenty-five minutes to ten. The delay in the Titanic's thirteen lifeboats. As the survivors came into the street a dead silence fell over the crowd that was assembled, and even the Press photographers refrained for a moment their bombardment.

STORIES BY SURVIVORS.

IMPORTANT STATEMENTS.

10.10 p.m.

The following statement by a committee of surviving passengers has been given to the Press:—

"We, the undersigned surviving passengers of the Titanic, in order to forestall any sensational and exaggerated statements, deem it our duty to give to the Press a statement of the facts which have come to our knowledge, and...

too many people in each boat to permit the same to be handled. On the Titanic the boat deck was about 75 feet above water, and consequently passengers were required to embark before the lowering of the boats, thus making the operation and preventing the taking on of the maximum number the boats should hold.

Sixthly: A. all items ought to be properly equipped with provisions, water, lamps, compass, lights, &c.

"Lifesaving boat drills should be more frequent and thoroughly carried out, and officers should be stationed at boat drill.

"Greater reduction in speed in fog and ice, as the danger of a collision actually occurs is liable the less.

"In conclusion we suggest an International Conference should be called, and we recommend the passage of identical laws providing for the safety of all at sea. We urge the United States Government to take the initiative as soon as possible."

The statement is signed by 'Mr. Samuel Goldenberg, chairman of the Passengers' Committee and twenty-five others.

REPORTED SUICIDE OF THE CAPTAIN.

It is asserted by one passenger of the Carpathia that Captain Smith committed suicide on the bridge of the Titanic before she went down, and that the Chief Engineer also committed suicide. This same passenger states that these Italians were shot dead in the struggle for lifeboats.

According to this circumstantial account of the captain's end, the revolver was wrested from his hands, but he broke away to the bridge and shot himself through the mouth.

Confusion in cabling the above story was erroneously included in statement by the committee of the surviving passengers.

ANOTHER GROUNDLESS RUMOUR.

Later - weather calm and clear: *Olympic* hastening to *Titanic*.
Later - *Baltic* within 200 miles and speeding to help.
New York 3.45 a.m. Cape Race telegraph says sinking by head - women being taken off by lifeboat.

ALL PASSENGERS DISEMBARKED (Reuters telegraph) New York - April 15 - a despatch from Halifax states that all the passengers of the *Titanic* had left the ship by 9.30 this morning.

STILL AFLOAT - MAKING FOR HALIFAX New York. April 15. - the *Montreal Star* reports that the *Titanic* is still afloat and making her way slowly to Halifax.

Even at this stage, however, there were hints that all was not well, and this is suggested in the rest of the *Evening News* report:

'WHEN TITANIC SHOULD MEET OLYMPIC - the *White Star Line* says it is very strange that the *Titanic's* sister ship *Olympic* which has a wireless installation of sufficient strength to send a message across the Atlantic should have sent us nothing.'

The truth emerged very quickly; the next morning the *Eastern Daily Press* had these grim headlines:

## 1600 LIVES LOST

## WORLD'S LARGEST LINER AT BOTTOM OF ATLANTIC

And in an editorial the paper commented: 'The powers of nature have prevailed and the leviathan of the deep lies at the bottom of the sea.' This high-flown language was the first indication of the subsequent tone of leader writing in papers, both national and local. The following day the editorial in the *Eastern Daily Press* thundered out its moral message: 'the most awful maritime catastrophe in the world's history ... the highest nobility of human nature asserted itself ... we have again been brought face to face with the stern fact that the forces of nature are inconceivable to the highest powers of man.' The reports of the tragedy were equally dramatic: 'The slowly accumulating evidence of the wireless messages has shattered popular faith in the indestructibility of modern floating palaces.'

In the same edition, the paper for the first time began to report news of 'local connections'. It has to be said that at no time did reporting in the Norfolk press lose sight of the wider issues to concentrate solely on more parochial news, as happened in

# MESSAGE FROM THE KING.

## SYMPATHY WITH THE BEREAVED.

## TELEGRAM TO WHITE STAR LINE.

The White Star Line have received the following telegram from the King and Queen :—

Sandringham,
Tuesday, 6.30 p.m.

The Managing Director,
White Star Line,
Liverpool,

The Queen and I are horrified at the appalling disaster which has happened to the Titanic and at the terrible loss of life. We deeply sympathise with the bereaved relatives, and feel for them in their great sorrow with all our hearts.

GEORGE R.I.

Queen Alexandra telegraphed to the White Star Line :

Sandringham, Tuesday.

It is with feelings of the deepest sorrow that I hear of the terrible disaster to the Titanic and of the awful loss of life. My heart is full of grief and sympathy for the bereaved families of those who have perished.

ALEXANDRA.

Aberdeen where a local paper's headline concerning the *Titanic* sinking read 'Local Man Lost in Accident at Sea.'! It was inevitable, however, that news of those with Norfolk connections would be avidly awaited by readers, and these were the first reports on Wednesday 17 April: 'Miss Estelle Stead, daughter of W. T. Stead, is this week presenting Shakespeare plays at Kings Lynn. She was on Tuesday greatly concerned about the safety of her father.' William T. Stead was one of the most famous of those who perished as a result of the disaster. He was a crusading journalist and editor of the *Pall Mall Gazette* who conducted campaigns against Siberian labour camps, slavery in the Congo, lack of housing for the poor, and child prostitution - this campaign led to his imprisonment for abduction, but also to the raising of the age of consent from thirteen to sixteen. He was sixty-four at the time of his death and had gained increasing notoriety as a result of his involvement with spiritualism. In a book entitled *Titanic - Psychic Forewarnings of a Tragedy* by George Behe, Stead has a whole chapter to himself!

Edward and Ethel Beane, and May Howard were mentioned in this local connections report as being passengers on the ship; a Mr T. King of Yarmouth, a master-of-arms who had moved to Southampton, was reported by his brother, Mr D. King, as being a member of the crew.

The *Eastern Daily Press* on the following day, Thursday, focused its attention on one the 'mysteries' surrounding the aftermath of the sinking - an early indication that 'mystery' was to be one of the enduring features of the whole story; this was the sub-heading and the report:

## MYSTERY OF THE CARPATHIA

## SILENCE AS TO DETAILS OF THE DISASTER

'A mystery apparently greater than how the *Titanic* met her fate forced itself to the front last night. Although the *Carpathia* was within the wireless telegraph zone for hours during the night, and both shore stations and relaying ships were able to send and receive numerous short messages to and from private individuals, not a word of description of the manner in which the doomed went to their deaths reached the shore.'

There were two reasons for this lack of information: on the *Carpathia* the wireless operator, Harold Cottam, had been joined by the *Titanic's* second operator, Harold Bird, who had survived the sinking. Together they were concentrating on sending the names of the survivors and their personal messages to New York via Cape Race, and they were refusing to answer any requests for information. The second reason for this lack of co-operation with the press in general is an early example of 'cheque-book journalism'. Both Cottam and Bride had been told by the Marconi office in New York that Guglielmo Marconi himself had arranged a deal with the *New York Times* to sell them the exclusive story of what had happened.

The headlines in the *Eastern Daily Press* on the following day, Friday 19 April, present a fascinating mixture of fact and speculation, so typical of accounts of what had happened.

## FULL STORIES BY TITANIC SURVIVORS
## HOW THE LINER WENT DOWN
## EXPLOSIONS AFTER CRASH
## BAND PLAYED 'NEARER MY GOD'
## REPORTED SUICIDE OF THE CAPTAIN
## HEARTRENDING SCENES AND AMAZING ESCAPES
## HOW THE BOATS WERE FILLED

After some vivid accounts of which the following is typical, 'The *Titanic* was ripped from stem to stern by a gigantic mass of ice, which tore her along the side as though by a huge can-opener', the article goes on to deal with more mundane local news:

## A NORTH WALSHAM SURVIVOR

'An additional list of survivors published this morning contains the name of Mary (sic) Howard. This is the name of the young woman who was going out from North Walsham.'

Saturday's paper had the same mixture of international and local news: 'There never has been, and probably there never will be again, so tragic a story of disaster at sea. 126 French emigrated on the *Titanic* - none arrived there safely ... Mrs G. Clarke of 33

Bond Street, Dereham Road, Norwich, received the following telegram from her daughter, Mrs Beane: 'New York. Both arrived safely, *Carpathia*. Will write. Ethel.' Perhaps the Editor was thinking of the Beane's story when he wrote on the following Monday, 'This vast ocean tragedy has revealed so much true greatness of character that even amid our sorrow for the lost we may justly feel proud of our kin.'

Other matters of interest are recorded in the bi-weekly newspaper the 'Norwich Mercury'. These show that there was a public hunger for any scrap of news or any piece of speculation. The edition of Saturday 27 April 1912 had a full-page article which included the following sub-headings:

### £10,000 OF FILMS LOST

'Mr Hamerstein of the London Opera House stated that on board was Mr Harris, a friend of his, who told him that he was taking back with him the moving films of the *Miracle* which he had secured for £10,000 and a royalty. These had all been lost.

### WHILE THE BAND PLAYED

One of the most striking pieces of heroism was that of the bandsmen who took their places on deck and played while the *Titanic* sank.

There were only eight members of the orchestra, their leader being Wallace Hartley, a young musician of Dewsbury, thirty-four years of age.

### FATE OF THE POST OFFICE SORTERS

The postal sorters aboard the *Titanic* completely disregarded their own safety when the vessel struck, and began to carry the 200 sacks of registered mails to the upper deck from the mail room and decks below. As the vessel was sinking they appealed to the stewards to help them save the mails. There were four sorters. Two were Englishmen, Mr E. D. Williamson and Mr Jago Smith, both of Southampton. The other two were Americans. They continued their work to the last. All of them were lost is the information which has reached the American Postmaster-General.'

Later reports dealt with the crew of the *Olympic* leaving the ship and refusing to sail because of insufficient lifeboats, and the

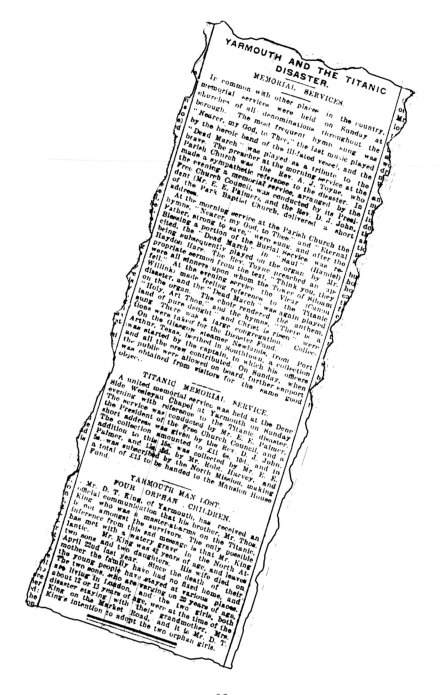

## YARMOUTH AND THE TITANIC DISASTER.

### MEMORIAL SERVICES.

In common with other places in the country, memorial services were held on Sunday at churches of all denominations throughout the borough. The most frequent hymn sung was "Nearer, my God, to Thee," the last music played by the heroic band of the ill-fated vessel, and the "Dead March" was played as a tribute to the brave. The preacher at the morning service at the Parish Church was the Rev. A. J. Toyne, who made a sympathetic reference to the disaster. In the evening a memorial service, arranged by the Free Church Council, was conducted by its President (Mr. E. E. Palmer), and the Rev. D. J. John, of the Park Baptist Church, delivered a short address.

At the morning service at the Parish Church the hymns, "Nearer, my God, to Thee," and "Father, strong to save," were sung, and after the Blessing a portion of the Burial Service was cited, the "Dead March" played on "Saul" (Handel) being subsequently played in the organ. Mr. Haydon Hare. The Rev. Toyne preached an appropriate sermon from the text, "Think you, the Vicar of Siloam were all sinners upon whom the Tower of Siloam fell." At the evening service the Vicar of Siloam, made feeling reference to the Titanic disaster, and the "Dead March" was again played on the organ. The choir rendered the anthem, "Holy, Art Thou," and the hymns, "There is a land of pure delight," and Christ is risen." were sung. There was a large congregation. Collections were taken for the Disaster Fund.

On the Glasgow steamer Newlands, from Port Arthur, Texas, berthed in Southtown, a collection was started by the captain, to which his officers and all the crew contributed. On Sunday, when the public were allowed on board, further support was obtained from visitors for the same good object.

### TITANIC MEMORIAL SERVICE.

A united memorial service was held at the Dene Side Wesleyan Chapel at Yarmouth on Sunday evening with reference to the Titanic disaster. The service was conducted by Mr. E. E. Palmer, the President of the Free Church Council, and a short address was given by the Rev. D. J. John. The collection amounted to £11 6s. 10d., and in addition to this 15s. was collected by Mr. E. E. Palmer, and 13s. 2d. by Mr. Robt. Harvey, and 5s. was subscribed by the North Mission, making a total of £13 to be handed to the Mansion House Fund.

### YARMOUTH MAN LOST.

### FOUR ORPHAN CHILDREN.

Mr. D. T. King, of Yarmouth, has received an official communication that his brother, Mr. Thos. King who was a master-at-arms on the Titanic, is not amongst the survivors. The only possible inference from this sad message is that Mr. King has met with a watery grave in the North Atlantic. Mr. King was 42 years of age, and leaves two sons and two daughters. His wife died on April 22nd last year. Since the death of their mother the family have had no fixed home, the young people having stayed at various places. The two sons, who are working in London, are about 12 or 13 years of age, and the two girls, both living in Yarmouth at the time of the disaster staying with their grandmother, Mrs. King, on the Market Road, were at the time of Mr. D. T. King's intention to adopt the two orphan girls.

60

progress of the Smith and Marsey inquiries. As late as the 28 April, the *Mercury* was still carrying stories such as the following:

## THE TITANIC DISASTER

## STATEMENT BY THE MASTER OF THE CALIFORNIAN

'Captain Stanley Lord, late Master of the S. S. *Californian* has sent to the newspapers a long letter, calling attention to circumstances which he says Lord Mersey's Inquiry into the loss of the *Titanic* failed to elicit, and which he claims show that deductions which reflect upon his personal character as a seaman are entirely unfounded.' If he felt this was to be the end of the story he was sadly mistaken!

In later chapters I shall be looking at some of the charitable events organised to raise money for the Disaster Fund, and at mentions of memorial services. These highlight the general nature of the tragedy, but one item in the *Mercury* brings home the idea of personal, individual loss in a very poignant way:

## YARMOUTH MAN LOST

## FOUR ORPHAN CHILDREN

'Mr D. T. King of Yarmouth has received an official communication that his brother, Mr Thos. King, who was a master-at-arms on the *Titanic*, is not amongst the survivors. The only possible inference from this sad message is that Mr King has met with a watery grave in the North Atlantic. Mr King was 42 years of age, and leaves two sons and two daughters. His wife died on April 22nd last year. Since the death of their mother the family have had no fixed home, and the young people have stayed at various places. The two sons, who are verging on 20 years of age, are living in London, and the two girls, both about 12 or 13 years of age, were at the time of the disaster staying with their grandmother, Mrs King on the Market Road, and it is Mr D. T. King's intention to adopt the two orphan girls.'

*Chapter Seven*

# Fund-raising Efforts

*'But what of the homes they have left,*
*The children forsaken and lone,*
*The widows who suffer and moan,*
*The lives of all gladness bereft? ...*
*God help us to pity them, too.'*

Harry Winter's poem, one of the many written in 1912 in the aftermath of the tragedy, sums up the feelings of many people who were appalled by the plight of the dependants of those who had been lost. The harsh rules of employment at sea meant that the pay of the crew who survived stopped at midnight on 14 April, and there was no provision for the wives and children of the 697 who had drowned. There was no hope that they could claim compensation through legal redress - even the richer American passengers and their relatives who sued had very limited success. Most of the crew lived in Southampton and the grief and suffering there was immense. An extract from the log of Northam Girls' School for 17 April 1912, sums this up: 'I feel I must record the sad aspect in school today owing to the Titanic disaster. So many of the crew belonged to Northam and it is pathetic to witness the children's grief; and in some cases faith and hope of better news. The attendance is suffering.' 125 children in the School had lost their fathers, but Northam was just one of the districts in Southampton which had suffered in this way. A local newspaper reported: 'Two-thirds of the crew of the *Titanic* were Southampton men, and I am told that today there are probably 500 homes robbed of the chief breadwinner.'

A wave of sympathy swept the nation, and a national *Titanic* Relief Fund was set up by the Lord Mayor of London, Sir Thomas Crosby. It eventually raised £413,000, equivalent to over twenty million pounds today. Great events were staged in London,

## ASSISTING THE "TITANIC" FUND.

The audience at the grand concert in the Thatched Assembly Rooms on Thursday evening, with the object of enhancing the "Daily Telegraph" fund in aid of the widows and orphans of those who met their untimely deaths in the recent Titanic disaster, was not perhaps as large as one would expect, never-theless the promoters hope to forward £10 to the fund. Primarily, the project was taken in hand by Miss Ella Pearce, and she was ably assisted in providing an excellent programme by Miss Edith Collins, Miss Ada Mullins, Miss Hallam, Mr. D. J. Stuart Chapman, Mr. B. A. Colman, and Mr. J. W. Hallam. The services of all the artistes were gratuitous, and the ac-companists were Mr. D. J. Stuart Chapman, and Mr. Arthur Olorenshaw. Messrs. A. J. Caley and Son, Ltd., presented chocolates with the object of helping the proceeds. The pro-gramme was as follows:—Pianoforte duet, "The Policeman's Holiday" (Ewing), Miss Ruth Mahony and Mr. D. J. Stuart Chapman; tableau vivant, scene from "The Merry Wives of Windsor," Mrs. J. Aubrey Blake, Miss Edith Collins, and Mr. J. Mahony; song, "Best of all" (Moir), Miss Mildred Rix; song, "Mary of Argyle," (S. Nelson), Mr. Geo. Beeston; song, "Sunshine and storm" (Simpson), Miss Edith Hindes; umbdella dance, "Tommy" (Kipling), Mr. Mills; recitation, "A common little girl," (Monckton), Miss Ida Mullins; tableau vivant, "Queen Phillipa interceding for the Burghers of Calais," Mrs. Aubrey Blake, Miss Edith Collins, Miss Lottie Hallam, Miss Cecil Varnon, H. W. Crowe, T. Betts, Messrs. Moore, J. Walsh, B. Garnham, C. S. Ashurst, M. Moore, Dawson, and others; song, "The magic month of May" (Newton), Miss Mildred Rix; old English gavotte, the Misses Phyllis Howes, Ida Hallam, Ruth Mahony, Idn Mullins, Tony Neal, M. and K. Ranson, and D. Topham; gavotte song, "A hundred years ago," Mr. Geo. Beeston; conjuring by Professor Lindren; song, "Good-bye" (Tosti), Mr. Ber-nard A. Colman; song, "Sometimes" (Rubens), Miss Ida Mullins, assisted by, Mr. Cecil Var-non; song, "The vicar's song" (Sullivan), Mr. A. G. Ballard; duet, "The day is done" (Lohr), Miss Edith Hindes, and Mr. Harry Mills; sketch, "The Duet," Miss Ruth Mahony and Mr. Cecil Varnon.

including a 'Dramatic and Operatic Matinee' at the Royal Opera House, Covent Garden on 14 May. Stars who gave their services included Sarah Bernhardt, Pavlova, Clara Butt and Vesta Tilley. Ushers and usherettes were recruited from the ranks of the aristocracy. In the audience were their Majesties King George V and Queen Mary. Ten days later at the Royal Albert Hall 'the greatest professional orchestra ever assembled' took part in 'The *Titanic* Band Memorial Concert' - with 500 performers from eight orchestras.

On a humbler scale, but with the same sympathy and earnestness, were the fund-raising efforts here in Norfolk; these must have been typical of many such events throughout Great Britain. It is interesting to focus on two concerts in Norwich, as they provide an insight into popular taste and examples of honest reporting which is not afraid to point to some lack of support for the performers! On 11 May the *Norwich Mercury* carried this report under the headline

ASSISTING THE "TITANIC" FUND:

'The audience at the grand concert in the Thatched Assembly Rooms on Thursday evening, with the object of enhancing the *Daily Telegraph* fund in aid of the widows and orphans of those who met their untimely deaths in the recent *Titanic* disaster, was not perhaps as large as one would expect, nevertheless the promoters hope to forward £10 to the fund. Primarily the project was taken in hand by Miss Ella Pearce ... the services of the artistes were gratuitous. Messrs A. J. Caley and Son, Ltd, presented chocolates with the object of helping the proceeds.' There were twenty varied items which included: a tableau vivant scene from *The Merry Wives of Windsor*, an umbrella dance, a recitation of 'Tommy' by Rudyard Kipling, another tableau vivant *Queen Phillipa interceding for the Burghers of Calais*, an old English gavotte, conjuring by Professor Lindrea, *The Vicar's Song* (Sullivan) and a sketch entitled *The Duet*.

Much more successful were the efforts of those at Norwich Hippodrome in the first week of May 1912. On Wednesday, 24 April the *Eastern Daily Press* had announced that there would be a special performance of a variety bill on Wednesday 1 May at 7 o'clock, with the entire proceeds going to the *Titanic* Disaster

*The Thatched Assembly Rooms, Norwich*

Fund. The performers would include 'the famous Australian entertainer' Albert Whelan, and 'the world-famous boy-juggler' Frank Hartley. Later the Band of the 16th Lancers was added to the list of those who were due to appear. The evening was to be 'under the distinguished patronage and presence of the Right Honourable the Lord Mayor and the Worshipful Sheriff'. On 2 May the paper reported that 'the house was thronged to its entire capacity'. A full report of this typical fund-raising effort appeared the next week in the *Norwich Mercury*.

## NORWICH HIPPODROME CONTRIBUTION

'The effort which is being made at the Norwich Hippodrome in aid of the Titanic Disaster Fund came to a culminating point on Wednesday night, when the entire proceeds of the first performance were devoted to the fund, and a collection was taken at each house in accordance with a practice which is being continued throughout the week. The Lord Mayor and the Lady Mayoress (Mr and Mrs H. J. Copeman) gave their patronage and were present in person. At the close of the performance Mr F. W. Fitt went to the footlights and made his acknowledgements on behalf of his partner, Mr E. H. Bostock and himself. He said that the takings amounted to £50 7s. 3d.; the collection realised £9 1s. 5½d., and this, with the collections taken on Monday and Tuesday, £9 16s. 5½d., made up a total of £69 5s. 2d. The collection at the second house amounted to £4 15s. 1d., thus making the total to Wednesday night £74 0s. 3d.' (£3,700 at today's values)

Our only evidence of the many other opportunities to contribute to the Fund comes in occasional references in the papers. Typical of this is a letter in the 'Eastern Daily Press of 4 May 1912:

## TITANIC FUND AT BUNGAY RACES

### Letter to the Editor from HARRY CLARE

'I take this opportunity of thanking those ladies and gentlemen who so kindly subscribed to the Lord Mayor's Titanic Fund at the recent Bungay races, and to inform them that the donations amounted to £33 13s.' (£1,650). Although Bungay is just over the border in Suffolk, I am sure there were Norfolk contributors

*The Hippodrome, Norwich*

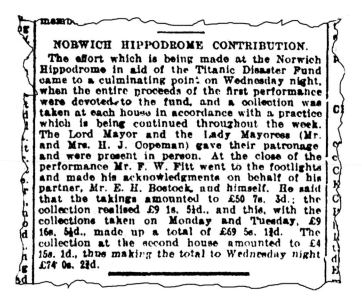

NORWICH HIPPODROME CONTRIBUTION.

The effort which is being made at the Norwich Hippodrome in aid of the Titanic Disaster Fund came to a culminating point on Wednesday night, when the entire proceeds of the first performance were devoted to the fund, and a collection was taken at each house in accordance with a practice which is being continued throughout the week. The Lord Mayor and the Lady Mayoress (Mr. and Mrs. H. J. Copeman) gave their patronage and were present in person. At the close of the performance Mr. F. W. Fitt went to the footlights and made his acknowledgments on behalf of his partner, Mr. E. H. Bostock, and himself. He said that the takings amounted to £50 7s. 3d.; the collection realised £9 1s. 5½d., and this, with the collections taken on Monday and Tuesday, £9 16s. 5½d., made up a total of £69 5s. 1½d. The collection at the second house amounted to £4 15s. 1d., thus making the total to Wednesday night £74 0s. 2½d.

to this fine total - so generous that it suggests that there were some substantial winnings that day!

Further contributions were made at the many memorial services held throughout the county. Four extracts will show something of the depth of feeling at these services - two in Norwich and two in Yarmouth. From the *Eastern Daily Press* on Monday, 22 April we have:

## THE TITANIC DISASTER

## PULPIT REFERENCES AT NORWICH CATHOLIC CHURCH

'An eloquent sermon was preached yesterday at the High Mass at 11 a.m. from the pulpit of St John's Catholic Church before a large and sympathetic audience by the Rev. H. S. Mulligan. "Millionaires and steerage passengers; men of letters and men without learning; men and women in the prime of life, young men and maidens in the heyday of youth, children with their feet on the threshold of life, old people tottering on the brink of the grave. To one and all the summons went forth - Cease! Your life's work is done".'

Two days later the 'Mercury' reported:

## YARMOUTH AND THE TITANIC DISASTER

## MEMORIAL SERVICES

'In common with other places in the country, memorial services were held on Sunday at churches of all denominations throughout the borough. The most frequent hymn sung was 'Nearer, my God, to Thee', the last music played by the heroic band of the ill-fated vessel, and the 'Dead March' was played as a tribute to the brave. The preacher at the morning service at the Parish Church was the Rev. A. J. Toyne, who made a sympathetic reference to the disaster.

At the evening service the Vicar (Canon Willink) made feeling references to the *Titanic* disaster, and the *Dead March* was again played on the organ. The choir rendered the anthem, *Holy, Art Thou*, and the hymns *There is a Land of Pure Delight* and *Christ is Risen* were sung. There was a large congregation. Collections were taken for the disaster fund. In the evening also a memorial service, arranged by the Free Church Council, was conducted by its President (Mr E. E. Palmer), and the Rev. D. J. John, of the Park Baptist Church, delivered a short address. The collection amounted to £11 6s. l0d., and in addition to this 15s was collected by Mr E. E. Palmer and 13s 2d. by Mr Robt. Harvey, and 5s. was subscribed by the North Mission, making a total of £13 to be handed to the Mansion House Fund. (£650) On the Glasgow steamer *Newlands*, from Port Arthur, Texas, berthed in Southdown, a collection was started by the captain, to which his officers and all the crew contributed. On Sunday, when the public were allowed on board, further support was obtained from visitors for the same good object.'

In the *Norfolk Chronicle* for May 4th a brief report stated that: "The offertories at Norwich Cathedral on Sunday were devoted to the Mansion-house Fund for the relief of the sufferers of the *Titanic* disaster. The Dean in his sermon commented that 'they died like heroes, giving their lives when the demand came for sacrifice'."

This sacrifice and the sheer scale of the tragedy had obviously touched the hearts of many in Norfolk; the extracts above represent just a few of those which could be cited to show this sympathy and generosity. The main relief fund was administered under the direction of the Mansion House council and executive committee in Lond on, with the help of local committees in Southampton, Liverpool and London. In the book *Titanic Voices - The Story of the White Star Line, Titanic and Southampton*, we learn of some of the recipients of grants from the fund: 'That a grant of £25 be made to enable Mrs Bristow to take her children to the seaside.'

'That Richard Edge (son aged 14) be apprenticed to Messrs Dixon Bros and Hutchinson (Marine Engineers Woolston) for a period of 5 years at a premium of £30.'

Beatrice Stagg, whose husband Jack was lost, received a letter in January 1913, informing her that she would receive relief - 15/6 per week, plus 3/- for her child, the allowance to be terminated automatically on re-marriage.

In 1953 it was reported that since 1912 the sum of £671,458 had been paid out in grants to dependants - more than one and a half times the amount originally subscribed by the public. In 1954 widows received an increase of 4/- per week, and in 1959 it was decided to wind up the fund, converting it into annuities for the remaining dependants.

The money subscribed in Norfolk in 1912 was well used; apart from the Yarmouth connections there were no direct links between dependants and the people of Norfolk which is a further testimony to the generosity of those who had no personal interest and yet gave willingly.

# Chapter Eight

# Remembering the Brave - Two Local Poets

**'They live in hearts that love them well,
And they grace Britannia's story.'**

The loss of the *Titanic* inspired a great deal of poetry, as writers tried to capture something of the drama, poured out their sympathy and found important moral lessons in the tragedy. The *New York Times*, which received a flood of verse offerings advised amateurs that 'to write about the *Titanic* a poem worth printing requires that the author should have something more than paper, pencil, and a strong feeling that the disaster was a terrible one.'

The magazine *Current Literature* commented 'we do not remember any other event in our history that has called forth such a rush of song in the columns of the daily press.' In England Thomas Hardy made a fine contribution to *Titanic* literature in his poem *The Convergence of the Twain*, written as an introduction to the programme of the Covent Garden Memorial Concert on 14 May. Volumes of poems soon appeared in print, such as the work *Poetical Tributes on the Loss of the Titanic*, edited by a leading Freemason, Chas. F. Forshaw, LL.D. Arranged in alphabetical order of authors, it begins with Helen Abercromby praising the ship's orchestra:

> *'They play, no thought of self,
> That noble, martyr band!
> Courage to comrades lending,
> Heroes, they bravely stand!'*

to John Young's alliterative musings:

*'Could we now weave a wreath with the deep seaweed,*
*'Neath the wave where the dear ones lie,*
*We would fain mark the spot, lest the dead be forgot,*
*For a lesson they taught, "how to die".'*

Two poems by Norfolk writers provide an interesting addition to these collections of verse tributes. Both were written by ordinary people, literary amateurs, who felt moved to commemorate the tragedy in a permanent form, and who found local publishers willing to print their thoughts.

On 21 April 1912, only six days after the sinking, Mrs Clarissa Green of 84 Gladstone Street, Norwich (not far from the home of Ethel Clarke/Beane) published *An Appeal on behalf of the Widows and Orphans through the loss of the 'Titanic', April 15th, 1912*. It cost one penny, and stated 'Net profits will be handed to the Widows' and Orphans' Fund.'

The poem has twelve verses and an epilogue, and begins with a statement of the situation:

*'Again Great Britain mourns*
*At another crushing blow;*
*A mighty ship, so nobly planned,*
*Has gone to the depth below.'*

The writer points out that the ship was said to be 'unsinkable':

*'Splendidly was she built,*
*So compact and so strong;*
*"UNSINKABLE" - she cannot sink,*
*Was the verdict passed along.'*

She attempts to give comfort to those who are sorrowing:

*'The widows and the orphans*
*Will not cry for help in vain,*
*For every true and loyal heart*
*Will share their grief and pain.'*

In a change of stanza form the Epilogue verse which follows a quotation from the book of Revelation sums up the poet's hope:

*'I trust these few lines in your deep bitter grief*
*May bring you some comfort and give you relief ...'*

It would be interesting to know if any 'widow' or 'orphan' ever saw the poem and how much it raised for the fund.

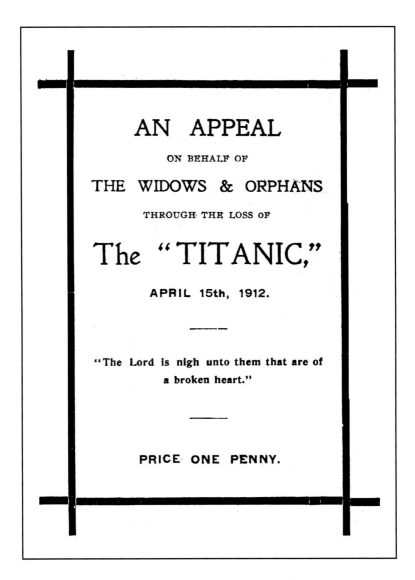

AN APPEAL

ON BEHALF OF

THE WIDOWS & ORPHANS

THROUGH THE LOSS OF

The "TITANIC,"

APRIL 15th, 1912.

———

"The Lord is nigh unto them that are of
a broken heart."

———

PRICE ONE PENNY.

Mrs Green's ballad style, with its easy rhyme-scheme, was a favourite vehicle for *Titanic* poems, and the four-line stanza provided the basis for the fifty-eight verses in the poem *The Wreck of the Titanic* published in 1912 by a poet from Old Catton, Arthur Futter. He ran a small chapel on North Walsham Road, and was in his late thirties when he heard the news of the sinking. His eight-page poem is a mixture of narrative and moral comment which reveals a detailed knowledge of the events which had occurred.

*'At last in March, nineteen-nought-nine,*
*The keel was laid …*
*Until the ship, all nice and even,*
*Was launched in May, nineteen-eleven …*
*And when in April, nineteen-twelve,*
*She started on a voyage sure; …*
*Of nations numerous were there*
*With millionaires not a few.'*

Arthur Futter writes about the captain of another ship who 'warned them of some ice at sea', and repeats an early accusation that:

*'For record-making they were bound,*
*Upon this maiden voyage round.'*

He contrasts those 'Who worshipped God on high' on Sunday, 14 April with those who 'Lived a life of ease and pleasure', and points the moral:

*'And man's great power is weak indeed*
*When God's great powers intervene.'*

He describes the collision with an iceberg, 'a mighty terror of the deep', talks about 'loving partings on the deck', and then mentions the wireless operators, Phillips and Bird, by name, as 'the "wireless" is brought into use.' We learn of Bandmaster Hartley who calls his men and they 'play sweet strains' as 'they at their posts do still remain'. In the final part of the poem the writer reflects on the fact that 'sixteen hundred lives were lost that night upon that mighty ship', and then considers some of the spiritual implications of the story. Some will question God's kindness in allowing 'such fateful things to occur', but 'Man disobeys the laws of God, then complains when He sends the rod.' In fact, men are to blame, not God.

*'And if the men upon that ship,*
*Of warning giv'n had taken heed,*
*Had sailed with caution 'mid the ice,*
*Shut down the steam and slacken'd speed,*
*Such tragedy had not occurred.'*

# THE WRECK

OF

# THE "TITANIC"

A POEM

BY

A. FUTTER

1912

NORWICH

C. G. GALLPEN, PRINTER, 10, POTTERGATE

His conclusion deals with our responsibility to others - 'life alone cannot be lived, for influence o'er others we have', and then reminds us that we should 'serve the Lord, and Him alone' so that 'We may with Him at last appear'.

We may be amused by the simplicity of this poem, by its sentimentality and by its lack of literary polish, but we should be impressed by its knowledge and understanding of what happened, and by its concern for human welfare. Perhaps its words rang through that small chapel on North Walsham Road, Old Catton; I am sure that the author would be surprised to hear that his thoughts are remembered at the end of the century.

In his study *Titanica - The Disaster of the Century in Poetry, Song and Prose* Steven Biel writes: 'None of the verse is worthless. Across the years, its turgidness and unoriginality seem more poignant than irritating: reflections of a powerful impulse to make sense of the senseless, to recast the shocking and unknown in terms of the comfortable and known.' The Norfolk poems provide a small contribution to this outpouring of feeling.

# Chapter Nine

# Myths, Memories and Models

## *'The night lives on.'*

In his book Steven Biel comments on the widespread impact of the disaster, from the early days when it was seen as a metaphor for divine judgement, for class, gender and race relations and for other battles of the day to the end of the century when 'the *Titanic* has resurfaced as a pop-culture phenomenon. Titanicmania - a Tony-winning Broadway musical, a TV mini-series, documentaries, recordings, books, newspaper and magazine articles, museum exhibits, CD-ROMS, Web-sites, and, of course, the Oscar-winning, record-breaking movie - reveals that the disaster speaks to us still.' The fascination of the story is mirrored in a number of ways in Norfolk, less pretentious perhaps but interesting in their own right.

Partly as a result of the many *Titanic* mysteries which have remained unsolved, the sinking has always attracted a number of myths. Locally this mainly takes the form of family stories about relatives who were passengers or members of the crew. These 'recollections' have been passed down to later generations, and it is very hard to shake the belief of family members who have grown up with the legend. In November 1996, Chris Stokes, a local reporter, wrote an article in the *Eastern Daily Press* asking for information about May Howard, the survivor from North Walsham. This article led to all the information provided by her niece, Gladys Whitworth, but the publication of my telephone number also resulted in a spate of calls claiming that relatives were on the ship. One claimant stated categorically that the ship was built in Barrow, that it sailed from Liverpool and that it called in at Devonport where a relative boarded as a maintenance worker! The fact that I supplied contradictory accurate information did not shake the caller's beliefs. In a number of cases I checked the lists of the lost and saved and there was no mention of the names given to me by families - again, I suspect that the family myths remain unshaken, much as it is impossible to persuade teenage fans of Leonardo di Caprio that no such person as Jack Dawson existed (the hero of the James Cameron film)!

Some of these 'myths' have found their way into the pages of local newspapers, as any mention of the *Titanic* has seemed a good story. On the 14 April 1973, the 61st anniversary of the sinking, the *Eastern Evening News* had one such story under the incorrect headline

'LAST SURVIVOR HAS ICY TITANIC MEMORIES'.

The article began 'Just 61 years ago today the great liner *Titanic* sank with the loss of 1500 lives after hitting an iceberg on her maiden voyage across the Atlantic.' So far, so good - but the next paragraph incorrectly states 'Of the 705 people who were saved, it is believed that there is now only one survivor, a 76-year-old Blundeston man, who was a 14-year-old bellboy on the *Titanic*.' I am not sure how many survivors were still alive in 1973, but as there are still five left in 1999 the claim that he was the last is obviously nonsensical!

In an interview, the 'survivor' gave graphic details of his 'ordeal'. 'The word came the boat was going down but everybody thought it was a joke, then she heaved over and over.' He produces a new theory as to the cause of the disaster: 'We heard afterwards that the iceberg was about as big as the British Isles and I think all the minerals in it must have affected the compasses and drawn us further north than the captain expected.' What might have alerted the journalist to the fact that the story was a complete fabrication was the man's account of his rescue: 'We were picked up in the afternoon of the next day by a Swedish or Belgian ship which landed us at Portland, Maine.' This one sentence manages to contain three basic errors - 'afternoon' should be morning, the 'Swedish or Belgian ship' should be the British-registered *Carpathia*, and 'Portland, Maine' should be New York! Age plays great tricks with the memory, and it is easy to see how some of these mistaken reminiscences come about.

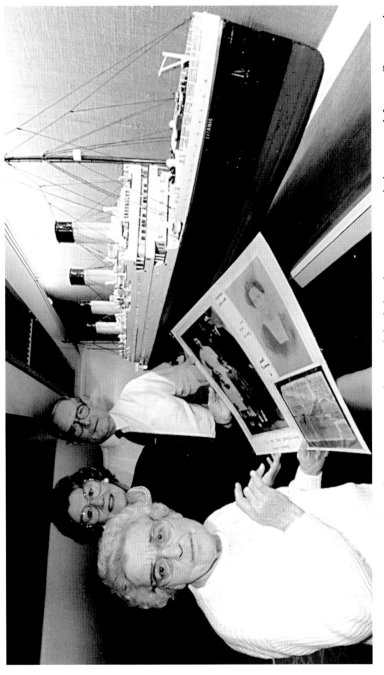

*Relatives of survivors of the disaster pose with a model of the ship at a special showing of James Cameron's film in January 1998 at the Odeon Cinema, Norwich. Left to right: Gladys Whitworth (niece of May Howard), Betty Terrell and Ted Clarke (neice and nephew of Ethel Beane)*

More recently, on 15 December 1997, another article featured an amazing lady, aged 99, who looked back on her life in Norwich, and included in her memories 'waving goodbye to her young schoolfriend Lucy, who set off for a new life on the doomed *Titanic* voyage.' Research into the passenger list has failed to locate any local girl named Lucy.

An example of how myths are created is provided by a story connected with one of the most important *Titanic* survivors - Second Officer C. H. Lightoller. He was washed overboard but managed to cling to an upturned submersible lifeboat, helping many others to survive. His part in the story is vividly portrayed by Kenneth More in the film *A Night To Remember*. In June 1940, at the age of 66, he took his 60-foot yacht, *Sundowner*, to Dunkirk as one of the fleet of little ships which rescued soldiers from the beaches. Previously he had crowded twenty-one people on board, but that day it brought back 130 men under constant fire.

After his death in 1952, *Sundowner* eventually found its way to a boatyard in Brundall - as Lightoller's biographer, Patrick Stenson, puts it 'under the caring ownership of Mr John Sapsford, a retired engineer from Norwich.' The yacht has now found a place in a maritime museum in Ramsgate, the port to which it returned from Dunkirk. This is factual information, and only a slight alteration produced the myth! Just after the new film was released in Norwich, I received a telephone call from Radio Norfolk, asking if I would answer a *Titanic* question on air. A caller had rung in, stating categorically that Lightoller had retired to Norfolk to live, and I was asked to confirm this. In fact, Lightoller, who tragically had lost two sons killed in action in World War II, eventually moved from the Medway to live in Middlesex. Perhaps we should not be surprised that the 'retirement' of *Sundowner* to Norfolk had become the retirement location of its owner.

Other memories have highlighted another and happier local side of the *Titanic* story. These concern people who were due to sail on the liner but for one reason or another did not go. As with the myths, these memories have become part of family folk-lore and surface whenever there is any publicity concerning

*"Sundowner" crossing Breydon Water*

*Motor yacht "Sundowner" in a quiet berth at Brundall Marina*

the tragedy. Three interesting Norfolk examples will show this: The *Great Yarmouth Mercury* for Friday 26 August 1994 had a report on its front page headed

## 'FATHER SAID NO TITANIC SAILING.'

'A Gorleston woman who was due to have sailed on the *Titanic* until her father insisted she stayed at home has died aged 104.

Neighbours this week paid tribute to Rachael Watker who was described as a 'lovely woman' and ' a great friend' by those who lived near her Cherry Road home.'

Two years later, after the publicity concerning May Howard, the following letter from Diana Brighton of Horstead appeared in the *Eastern Daily Press*.

## 'FAMILY JUST MISSED FATAL TITANIC TRIP'

'I wondered whether John Balls would be interested in the story of my family who, incidentally, were also from North Walsham.

My grandfather William Sampson Cork had previously emigrated to Canada and had established a home for his family.

My grandmother Jane and the three youngest of her seven children, Dorothy Ellen, John and Walter James (my father) were booked to sail on the *Titanic*, but as fate would have it James (Jimmy) went down with measles just before they were due to sail and consequently they were unable to take up their berth.

When news of the disaster broke my grandfather had not received the telegram my grandmother had sent, and believed them to be aboard, not knowing if they had survived or not ...

In conclusion, but for the grace of God and measles my brother and I might never have existed, and in turn Jimmy's seven grandchildren and two great-grandchildren.'

Reasons for not sailing are many and varied, but one of the most unusual is recounted in the *Eastern Evening News* on Wednesday 22 January 1997. In this article Derek James interviewed a Norwich octogenarian, Don Strivens. In one of his anecdotes Don tells us that his Aunt Elizabeth's first husband went to America to seek his fortune, and in 1912 she had been about to join him when she had a dream. 'The night before she was due to begin her journey she said an angel appeared to her and told her not to go,' recounted Don. 'The name of the ship she had been due to sail on was the *Titanic*.'

One of the abiding mysteries connected with the sinking has been the question of the fate of the lifeboats. One theory is that thirteen of the sixteen main lifeboats were taken on board the *Carpathia* and sent to a New York shipyard. They were then brought back to England and installed in time for the *Olympic's* next sailing to New York. They remained in service until the *Olympic* was broken up in 1936. The lifeboats were auctioned off together with the ship's fittings. At intervals since 1936 claims have been put forward for ownership of these boats, often with attempts to sell them as expensive souvenirs.

The situation has been complicated by the construction of replicas for films - these in turn have reappeared as 'originals'. In an article for an American magazine, Chris Crowther, a Norfolk expert on the lifeboats, wrote: 'Even those replicas, made for the film *A Night To Remember* would be of some interest. But nothing compares to the real thing. And that "real thing" might be lying right now in some fog-shrouded English creek. To the *Titanic's* survivors, those lifeboats must have been the most precious things on earth. Who could guess at what one would be worth if it were found now?' With the Broads as such an integral part of the Norfolk landscape, it is not surprising that one such a claim has been put forward for a local 'fog-shrouded creek'. In a boatyard at Upton Dyke are the remains of a wooden boat which once had two metal White Star badges attached. The badges are still there in a workshop, and in the woodwork of the boat we can still see that information was cut which states that her capacity was 58 persons.

In an article in the *Yarmouth Mercury* in 1988 the writer of *Through the Porthole* wrote that 'The *Girl Madge II* was a converted ship's lifeboat which was regularly berthed in the Yare at Yarmouth so her owner, Colin Angel, could use her for winter sea-angling trips, but kept in Upton Dyke at other times.' He added, 'You cannot help but a thrill of excitement to learn that there is a possibility - and it would be quite wrong to put it into any higher category - that for many years in the Yarmouth area there has been a survivor of the great ship: a lifeboat which

*Lifeboats from the Titanic at the White Star Pier, New York, shortly after being removed from the Carpathia*

*Pat Goreham inspects the White Star Line insignia on
The Girl Madge II*

helped to ensure that the death-toll was no higher'. The local
historian, Geoffrey Goreham, investigated the claim, based on
the fact that the *Girl Madge II* was exactly the right size and
weight. But he failed to unravel the mystery. With the help of
Richard Horsley at the Upton Yard, Chris Crowther and I made
further investigations, again with no conclusive outcome. The
showing of the Cameron film prompted further interest, and on

*The Girl Madge II at Upton Dyke*

Friday 12 June 1998 *Through the Porthole* took up the story again under the headline

'BOAT THE CENTRE OF TITANIC RIDDLE'.

Shortly after this, sadly, Geoffrey Goreham died, with the mystery still unsolved. Two months later in the *Yarmouth Mercury, Peggotty* wrote another article, this time headed

'TITANIC THEORY IS SINKING FAST':

'A suggestion aired in this column ten years ago - and resurrected recently - that a locally-based angling boat might have an exciting and historic past has probably been sunk as deep as the ill-starred luxury liner *Titanic* herself'. He then goes on to report that Kenneth Kent of Gorleston had supplied him with details of the history of the *Girl Madge II*. She was built at Great Yarmouth in 1924 and worked as a pleasure boat off Yarmouth Beach. Another maritime expert, Stephen Brewster Daniels, added further details and concludes, 'she could not have been on the *Titanic.*' This sounds conclusive but it is hard not to share with *Peggotty* his 'glimmer of hope' that the *Girl Madge II* was one of the lifeboats' - as he states, 'as yet there is no explanation for that White Star insignia on the side of the *Girl Madge II.* There is still hope, however slender.'

Yarmouth provides yet another unusual link with the *Titanic* story. After the 'May Howard' article in the *Eastern Daily Press* another octogenarian, Richard Berry, of Caister-on-Sea rang me to tell me about an unusual piece of cargo on board the ship. This was not only unusual, but in the light of what happened, highly ironic. Mr Berry worked for Grout and Company, Textile Manufacturers, who made black silk mourning crape. Documents from the firm's records show that during the course of a meeting of the board of directors in April 1912, the company secretary, Mr. T Hall, reported that two cases of their material had been lost in the *Titanic* disaster. The value of the two cases was £108 but was covered by insurance. In 1912 the value of £108 would have purchased about 700 to 800 yards. The cargo manifest of the *Titanic* shows there were three cases of mourning crape on board and were bound for Spielmann and Company in America. The extra case was probably purchased from another

*An engraving of Grout & Co.'s factory at St Nicholas Road Mill, Great Yarmouth, in 1912*

*The mourning crape packing and despatch department of Grouts in 1912*

manufacturer, such as Courtaulds, or it may have been a Norwich manufacturer as at that time Francis Hine and the Norwich Crape Company were both making mourning crape. I am sure that Thomas Hardy would have appreciated the irony here - perhaps the mourning crape accompanying bodies to their watery grave might have found its way into his great poem *The Convergence of the Twain*!

Since 1998 a group of *Titanic* enthusiasts have met as the Norfolk *Titanic* Association, and the variety of strands of interest is well illustrated by their expertise in different aspects of the subject. One member who has featured in the press, both local and national, is Robin Burrows from Norwich, an expert model-maker. He has made a number of models of the ship, but the one which captured the headlines was his impressive eight-foot model which took 6,000 hours to build over five years and cost £250 in materials. As the latest film reached local screens in January 1998, Robin's model appeared in newspapers from The *Eastern Evening News* to *The Sun*, and on television. The story concerned the fact that having completed the large and highly-detailed model in his shed Robin had no room for it in the house!

*Robin Burrows from Norwich with his eight-foot model of the Titanic*

The resulting publicity brought offers to exhibit it locally and nationally - at the time of the showing of the film in Norwich it was on display in Jarrolds Department store and caused a great deal of interest, as did a smaller brass model in their window. It was on display, too, at a special showing of *Titanic* at the Odeon in Norwich attended by relatives of the Norfolk survivors. It hit the headlines again when it appeared at a special charity ball at the Stakis Hotel in September 1998, accompanied by a replica brass bell given to Robin by his late father. The bell was stolen, but a newspaper plea from Robin resulted in the bell being sent back to the hotel by taxi - as the Evening News headline writer put it - 'BELL APPEAL IS A RINGING SUCCESS'.

One of the most fascinating features of *Titanic* research is that new stories are always emerging as people delve into family records and organisations realise their links with the tragedy. One recent poignant memory which has been revived is that of a seventeen year old pantry boy, Frederick Humby, who died on the ship. A caller to Radio Norfolk alerted listeners to the fact that Barnardo's were trying to trace a stained-glass window which was erected in his memory. The

*Frederick Humby, the Barnardo's Boy who perished on the Titanic*

story was taken up in the *Eastern Daily Press* by reporter Rebecca Holmes in a feature headed 'Hunt for Stained-Glass Tribute To Titanic Hero'. The local link is provided by the fact that Frederick was educated at the Barnardo's sponsored Watts Naval Training School in the hamlet of County School in the centre of Norfolk. He was there for two years until he signed on aboard the *Titanic* in 1912. His friends were convinced that he died heroically helping to save others on the night of 14 April 1912, and so they decided to commemorate him with a stained-glass window in the school's chapel. It was inscribed 'To

*The missing Barnardo's stained-glass window (left panel)*
*commemorating Frederick Humby who was lost on the Titanic*

the Glory of God and in memory of Frederick Humby, a boy hero, who perished on board the SS *Titanic* - 15 April, 1912, aged 17 years'. When the chapel was closed and then demolished in 1953 the window was transferred to the chapel at Barnardo's headquarters in Stepney. This chapel was also demolished in 1968, and since then there has been no trace of the window, although there is a possibility that it was moved to an Essex Church. We finish therefore with a memory and a mystery, which reflects so well the human stories behind this epic tragedy.

# Conclusion

The appeal of the *Titanic* remains undiminished after eighty-seven years - in fact it appears to be growing. A number of factors contribute to this phenomenon, and this short account of the links with Norfolk illustrates these in a small way. One important aspect of the sinking is that it combines the enormous - the global features and the sheer size of the tragedy - with individual stories which are full of emotion. The lives of the Norfolk survivors, and their links with important people, illustrate this juxtaposition in a telling way. The human stories are the foundation of our interest in the tragedy, and we can glimpse reality in what happened to Frank, Edward, Ethel, Ellen and May. Another absorbing aspect of the subject is the reaction of the people not themselves closely involved but nevertheless caught up in the emotional aftermath of the sinking. The treatment of the story by the local press, the response to the appeal for financial help for those in need and the outpouring of comment in prose and verse assist us as we try to understand what this impact was - to see this in a limited, local context adds to what we know of the world-wide reaction.

Above all, perhaps, the fascination of the story rests on the many mysteries which remain, and which are the subject of constant research. I hope that this book will make its own contribution to the solving of some of these mysteries, and I look forward to hearing additions to the stories I have told. Robert Ballard, after finding the wreck in 1985 was asked why the *Titanic* story is so compelling and enduring. He replied with a variety of factors, including the wealth of those aboard, the arrogance of those who thought the ship was 'unsinkable', the loss of innocent life, the heroes, the cowards, and he concluded with these words, 'It was a morality play acted out on the deck of the ship.' Norfolk provided some of the characters in the 'play' - and the county offers insights into the abiding appeal of the drama.

Nearer, my God, to Thee.
Nearer to Thee;
E'en though it be a cross
That raiseth me;
Still all my song shall be,
"Nearer, my God, to Thee.
Nearer to Thee".

*Other East Anglian titles available from*

**NOSTALGIA Publications**

### THE HOBBIES STORY
*Terry Davy*
Over 100 years of the history of the well known fretwork company

### LARN YERSALF NORTHAMPTONSHIRE
*Mia Butler and Colin Eaton*
A comprehensive guide to the Northamptonshire dialect

### LARN YARSELF SILLY SUFFOLK
*David Woodward*
A comprehensive guide to the Suffolk dialect

### LARN YARSELF NORFOLK
*Keith Skipper*
A comprehensive guide to the Norfolk dialect

### MIGHTA BIN WUSS
*Tony Clarke*
The hilarious adventures of the Boy Jimma

### TATTERLEGS FOR TEA
*David Woodward*
More Suffolk Dialect in Yarns and Verse

### KID'S PRANKS AND CAPERS
*Frank Reed*
Nostalgic recollections of childhood

### RUSTIC REVELS
*Keith Skipper*
Humorous country tales and cartoons

### MEMORIES OF NORFOLK CRICKET
*Philip Yaxley*
200 years of history of Norfolk Cricket